Life Skills for Women Living Alone

A 7-day Refreshment for Self-love,
Financial Wellness, and Security

Winnie Gold

LIFE SKILLS FOR WOMEN LIVING ALONE

Life Skills for Women Living Alone: A 7-Day Refreshment for Self-love, Financial Wellness, and Security

Copyright © 2023 Souls Press Limited
For inquiries related to orders or general information, please reach out to the publisher at info@soulspress.com.
All rights reserved.

No part of this book may be reproduced or transmitted in any form or by any means, electronic or mechanical, including photocopying, recording, or by any information storage and retrieval system, without permission in writing from the author, except in the case of brief quotations embodied in critical articles or reviews.

The author has undertaken comprehensive research to ensure the accuracy of the information presented at the time of publication; however, she cannot assume responsibility for any errors or omissions.
Published by Souls Press Limited

http://www.soulspress.co
ISBN : 978-1-7386088-1-2 (hardcover)
ISBN : 978-1-7386088-3-6 (paperback)
ISBN : 978-1-7386088-4-3 (eBook)

CONTENTS

BONUS PAGE 7

INTRODUCTION 9

CHAPTER ONE 17

    PREVENTATIVE MEASURES FOR HEALTH AND SAFETY 18

    YOUR "KEY" TO SUCCESS 19

    SIP SMART AND STAY HEALTHY 20

    BALANCING SECURITY AND HOSPITALITY 22

    SAFEGUARDING SAFETY THROUGH PRIVACY 23

    LOCKING UP WITHOUT BEING LOCKED IN 24

    THE LIFELINE IN YOUR POCKET 26

    DON'T LET ACCIDENTS CLIMB UP ON YOU 28

    SECURING YOUR FINANCE PRIVACY 29

    STAYING SAFE DURING POWER OUTAGES 31

    YOUR DAILY HEARTBEATS 32

    THE DISTRESS SIGNAL 33

CHAPTER TWO 37

    TROUBLESHOOT WI-FI PROBLEMS 39

    UNDERSTAND YOUR CIRCUIT BREAKER PANEL 41

    LOCATE THE WATER SHUT OFF VALVE 44

    RESOLVE AN UNUSUAL WATER BILL 45

    JUMP START A CAR 47

    UNCLOG A DRAIN OR THE SINK 49

    MAINTAIN A HANDYMAN LIST 51

    LEARN SOME FIRST AID SKILLS 53

    UPKEEP HOME APPLIANCES 55

LIFE SKILLS FOR WOMEN LIVING ALONE

    CHANGE A TIRE 57
    RAID OF BUGS 58

CHAPTER THREE **63**
    BUILD FINANCIAL STABILITY FOR A LIFETIME 65
    CALCULATE DISPOSABLE INCOME 67
    BUILD A RESERVE 69
    KEEP TRACK OF MONTHLY SPENDING 72
    MANAGE YOUR SPENDING 74
    STAY AWAY FROM WINDOW SHOPPING 78
    WATCH OUT FOR ONLINE SHOPPING 81
    BE MINDFUL ON MONTHLY SUBSCRIPTIONS 84
    MANAGE CREDIT CARD SPENDINGS 86
    SETTLE DEBTS AND REPAYMENT PROMPTLY 88
    SET REALISTIC FINANCIAL GOALS 90
    STAY IN CONTROL 93

CHAPTER FOUR **97**
    A SAD STORY 99
    SENSIBLE AND PROPER DIET 100
    NEVER SKIP A PROPER MEAL 104
    WORK-LIFE BALANCE 107
    REST AND SLEEP 110
    DEVELOP AN EXERCISE ROUTINE 114
    ASSOCIATE WITH POSITIVE FRIENDS 118
    MENTAL HEALTH AND WELL-BEING 122
    AVOID SOCIAL MEDIA WHEN FEELING DESPAIR 125

CHAPTER FIVE **129**
    WHO IS YOUR TRUE FRIEND? 132

- Our Commitment to a Friend 134
- The Inner Circle 137
- Our Support Network 141
- Cherish and Nurture Friendship 144
- Defend Your Friendship 147
- Be a Good Listener 149
- Allow Friends to Help 150
- Start of a Relationship 152
- Protect Yourself 153
- Your Digital Presence 156

CHAPTER SIX 161
- Prioritize Your Own Needs 164
- Focus Internally not Externally! 166
- Self-Care 168
- Childhood Experience 171
- Build Positive Self Image 175
- Self-Improvement 178
- Empower Yourself 181
- Pursue Your Dream 184
- Stand Up and Get Going 186

CHAPTER SEVEN 191
- Understand Yourself 193
- Your Inside Voice 196
- Let Go of Your Worry 198
- Exercise and Sports 199
- Picking Up a Hobby 201
- Hobby and Volunteerism 203
- Religion Related Volunteerism 206

LIFE SKILLS FOR WOMEN LIVING ALONE

LIFE PURSUIT	207
CONCLUSION	**210**
REFERENCES	**218**

BONUS PAGE

As an expression of gratitude for your purchase, I would like to offer you a comprehensive set of resources, including worksheets, checklists, and a financial health assessment tool. These valuable tools are specifically designed to help you effortlessly manage your budget, track your daily expenses, and so much more.

Scan the following QR code.
Alternatively, you may visit this website.
https://soulspress.com/opt-in-page-winnie-gold

ACKNOWLEDGEMENT

I would like to express my gratitude and sincere thanks to all my friends who generously contributed their personal stories and experiences to this book. Your willingness to contribute and share your insights has helped create a collection of narratives that is rich and diverse.

While your names have been altered to protect your privacy, your experiences and insights have made a profound impact on the content of these pages, and the essence of your stories remain true, allowing deep resonates with readers. I am deeply grateful for your trust, support, and the valuable contributions you have made to this project. Your stories have brought authenticity and inspiration to these pages, and I am honored to have had the opportunity to include them in this book. Thank you all for being a part of this incredible journey.

With heartfelt appreciation,

Winnie Gold

Introduction

Welcome to "Life Skills for Women Living Alone"! I'm glad to share with you my experiences accumulated throughout these years. As a woman who has spent most of my life living alone, I relish the freedom and autonomy that it provides, while also savoring the unique challenges and trials that come with the independence. Despite its difficulties, there is something liberating and empowering about making decisions for myself and taking control of my own life. It is an enriching experience that I wouldn't trade for anything.

From my twenties to my fifties, each stage has brought different experiences and skills. Living alone is enjoyable, but it comes with some inconvenience. Living alone is a double-edged sword. One can enjoy flexibility and freedom, but it can also be overwhelming at times. We have the freedom to live our lives as we please, make our own decisions, and enjoy the peace and quiet of our own private world. We have complete sovereignty over what music to play or not play. We have the choice to skip a meal or cook something fancy. On the other hand, we are constantly inundated with the responsibilities that come with independence – managing our finances, maintaining our homes, building and maintaining healthy lifestyles, protecting our own safety and well-being, etc.

Over the years, I have continued to learn and grow, adapting to new challenges and opportunities that come my way. Through this journey, I have developed a set of life skills that work well for me as well as for my close friends. We love to exchange tips and ideas, all with the aim of supporting each other in living a self-contained and sustainable life. That's why I wrote this book – I want to share these collective learning and experiences with more people like you!

Whether you're a young adult just starting out on your own

or a seasoned pro who has been living independently for years, this book is packed with practical tips and strategies that will help you thrive. I understand some of you are quick readers and could finish this book in a day or two. While I have intentionally structured it into 7 chapters, and I highly recommend treating it as a 7-day refreshment course. By spacing out your reading over the course of a week, you'll give yourself ample time to let the ideas and concepts sink in. This allows for reflection and deeper understanding, allowing you to apply these key concepts to your own unique lifestyle. Without further ado, please come and join me on this exciting journey of self-discovery and empowerment and let us learn and grow together!

How to Use this Book

When I first started living alone, I used to make silly mistakes, such as locking myself out in the winter wearing a pair of shorts. I used to feel sorry for myself; however, looking back now, I can't help but feel like I'm reading a joke book.

Back then, I wished there was a guidebook or someone to tell me all the tips and skills I needed. Those were the days, and now I am a life coach teaching my friends how to turn lemons into lemonade. This book is dedicated to all of us, to share my experiences and to help those who are on the same journey.

This book is organized into modular chapters, each covering an independent topic and offering practical tips and dos-and-don'ts that you can use to improve your daily life. Beyond just the practical advice, I've included anecdotes and real-life stories that will allow you to connect with and learn from the experiences of others. This book has been carefully crafted to be both easily digestible and engaging, equipping you with the tools and knowledge you need to thrive and take pride in your solo lifestyle.

No matter what you're looking for - whether it's advice on essential life skills, safety and security tips, good financial habits, building and maintaining friendship and a supporting network, or developing a sustainable and fulfilling lifestyle – I have something for you. This book is designed to help you take control of your life and invest in your own life-long well-being, providing you with a comprehensive toolkit of skills that will empower you to thrive on your own terms. So, if you're ready to join me, come and dive in and start exploring!

Below is an outline of the book.

Chapter One focuses on safety, highlighting the importance of protecting yourself from danger before it's too late. You can never be too careful, and this chapter will help you feel empowered and prepared.

In Chapter Two, you'll learn the fundamental life skills that every woman living alone requires, as well as tips and tricks for managing household issues.

Chapter Three delves into the realm of finances, exploring the importance of building good habits and financial stability to give you a sense of security and peace of mind. After all, the last thing you want is to feel vulnerable or uncertain about your financial future.

Chapter Four turns to the subject of health and mental well-being, acknowledging that physical and mental health can be major issues for women living alone. By building awareness and developing a sustainable lifestyle, you can take control of your health and well-being and prioritize your own needs.

Chapter Five explores the vital importance of friendship and relationships, reminding us that maintaining a support network is crucial for both our mental and physical health. Emotional support can be a lifeline during tough times, and this chapter offers insights and tips for building and maintaining healthy relationships with those around us.

Chapter Six is a profound exploration into the realm of self-love – a journey of discovering the infinite reservoir of compassion, acceptance, and appreciation that resides within each of us. In this chapter, we delve into the significance of nurturing our own well-being, embracing our unique qualities, and cultivating a deep sense of love and respect for ourselves. As we embark on this transformative path, we open ourselves up to a world of self-discovery, inner healing, and the realization that true happiness begins from within.

Chapter Seven talks about discovering new hobbies and passions. One of the joys of living alone is the freedom to explore new interests and hobbies. Chapter Seven invites you to embark on a captivating exploration of self-discovery and the pursuit of new passions. Chapter Seven guides us on a path of self-fulfillment and personal growth. With an open mind and a curious spirit, we discover the immense satisfaction that comes from discovering our passions and nurturing our souls.

Along with this book, I am providing you with a bonus set

of worksheets and checklists that I have personally used and found to be useful. I have also shared them with close friends who found them to be highly relevant too. My hope is that, by providing these resources, I can help you cultivate the skills and habits that will pay off in the long run. To access these resources, please subscribe to my email list. Instructions on how to redeem the bonus can be found on page 7.

Are you ready to begin the amazing journey of our solo lifestyle? If so, let's get going and start this amazing journey!

Chapter One

SAFETY FIRST

"Safety is not an intellectual exercise to keep us in work. It is a matter of life and death. It is the sum of our contributions to safety management that determines whether the people we work with live or die."

Sir Brian Appleton

LIFE SKILLS FOR WOMEN LIVING ALONE

As a woman living alone, your safety should always be a top priority. While it's important to enjoy the freedom and independence that come with living alone, it's equally important to remain vigilant and prepared for any potential dangers. This chapter focuses on the topic of safety, highlighting the importance of taking proactive measures to protect yourself from harm.

Preventative Measures for Health and Safety

The first piece of advice I would give is to always have a first aid kit and extra medications on hand. Always keep painkillers like paracetamol, cold and flu medications, bandages, antiseptic ointment, and any other medications or medical supplies you might require on hand. Accidents can occur at any moment, so having a fully stocked first aid kit is essential in an emergency. This advice is crucial especially when you are traveling.

Your "Key" to Success

Have you ever misplaced your keys and been locked out of your home? Some of us might have come across this frustrating and even scary situation, especially if it happens in the middle of the night or during bad weather. One chilly evening, I left my apartment to take out the trash, and when the wind shut the door, I realized I didn't have my keys. It was a freezing night, and I was only wearing a pair of shorts without any shoes. When I realized I couldn't get back into my apartment, panic quickly set in. Thankfully, my next-door neighbor was still awake, and I was able to use his phone to call a locksmith, who promptly arrived and let me back into my house.

This ordeal taught me a valuable lesson: never leave your

house without your keys on hand. A good piece of advice is to always check your purse or pockets before closing the door. If you have trouble keeping track of your keys, consider investing in a keyless system that uses access codes or fingerprints. In an emergency, entering a passcode can take 5 to 10 seconds, so I prefer fingerprint locks. However, if you live in a rental property, you may not be able to install one for yourself.

Under any circumstances, consider leaving a secondary set of keys with a nearby friend you trust. This is beneficial not only for gaining access during an emergency, but also for summoning assistance during an emergency.

Sip Smart and Stay Healthy

Being sick can be a very difficult experience when you live alone. Not only are you physically ill, but you may also be lonely and vulnerable because no one is looking after you. While it is impossible to avoid becoming ill entirely, there are steps you can take to reduce your risk. Eating a well-balanced and healthy diet, staying active, and getting enough sleep are all essential for good health. However, it is also important to be mindful of your alcohol consumption, as excessive alcohol consumption can result in a painful hangover that can leave you feeling miserable for hours or even days. So, if you must drink, do so in moderation, and always remember to stay hydrated. And if you do end up with a hangover, there are some simple steps you can take to alleviate your discomfort. Drinking plenty of water, getting plenty of rest, and taking over-the-counter pain relievers can all help relieve your symptoms and get you feeling better quickly. Remember that taking care of your health is critical when living alone, and by taking a few simple precautions, you can help to ensure that you stay healthy and happy even when you are sick.

Balancing Security and Hospitality

You are solely responsible for the safety and security of your home when you are living alone. It is critical to exercise caution when allowing strangers into your home, especially for deliveries or service calls. While most people are honest and trustworthy, it is critical to remain vigilant and take precautions to protect yourself and your home. Making it appear as if you're not living alone is a simple but effective way to deter potential intruders. When there is a service call, such as a plumber, I always give the impression of a male presence. I simply keep an extra pair of shoes or slippers near the front door. You could also leave a television on in the bedroom to give the impression that someone else is home. Another helpful suggestion is to keep a razor and an extra toothbrush in the bathroom to give the impression that you do not live alone. While these may appear to be minor precautions, they can help deter potential intruders and make you feel more secure in your own home. Remember, it's always better to err on the side of caution when it comes to your safety and security. Take the necessary precautions to keep yourself safe, and always trust your instincts if something doesn't feel right. If you remain vigilant and take precautions, you can enjoy the independence and freedom of living alone while also feeling secure and protected.

Safeguarding Safety Through Privacy

It's critical to be cautious about what you post on social media, especially when it comes to your location and living arrangements. It is especially important to be cautious when traveling when no one is at home. Sharing your travel plans on social media can invite burglars to target your home while you're gone. Furthermore, avoid posting too much information about your daily routine and habits, such as when you typically leave for work or return home. Potential intruders can use this information to plan a break-in. It's also critical to be aware of who you're sharing information with on the Internet. Accepting friend requests from strangers and sharing personal information with strangers should be avoided. Even seemingly insignificant details like your occupation or the fact that you live alone can put you at risk.

To protect yourself, consider adjusting your social media privacy settings to limit who can see your posts and information. You should also refrain from sharing your current location or posting photos until you have returned home. Remember that your safety and security of yourself is in your own hands. Take precautions to protect yourself and be cautious about what you share online.

Locking Up Without Being Locked In

I couldn't help but laugh out loud when Athena shared with me her story, but I could sense her frustration and fear that she was experiencing at the time.

Athena got trapped in her shower box when the glass door got stuck and could not be opened from the inside. She struggled for half an hour before realizing she needed to come up with a creative way to save herself. Using the faucet as a step, she climbed to the top of the shower box by holding onto the shower hose and eventually managed to climb out from the top.

As amusing as it may appear, Athena's experience teaches an important lesson: damaged door locks can pose a serious safety risk to those living alone. It's critical to keep your maintenance up to date, especially when it comes to your home's doors and locks.

If you are living in a house, a jammed door may not be a major inconvenience because you can still exit through other doors. However, if you live in an apartment, a broken lock and jammed door could be disastrous.

The Lifeline in Your Pocket

Keeping your phone close by can make a huge difference in unexpected health issues, accidents, or emergency situations. Monica shared with me a story about a recent Benign Paroxysmal Positional Vertigo (BPPV) attack. BPPV is an inner ear disorder that causes sudden and severe dizziness.

One morning, Monica woke up and tried to get out of bed, but she felt so dizzy that she immediately fell back into bed. She said her vertigo was so bad that she felt the whole world was spinning and the slightest motion made her feel very unwell and nauseous. Luckily, her phone was by her bedside, so she immediately called her sister to take her to the doctor.

If Monica hadn't had her phone nearby during her BPPV attack, she could have gone hours or even days without being able to seek medical attention. Imagine if this were a life-threatening situation; every minute would be crucial, and any delay could cost lives.

I understand that some health-conscious people suggest not keeping your mobile phone nearby while sleeping due to radiation. However, I strongly suggest having your phone charged and close by at all times. You never know when you might need to call for assistance or help. Monica's experience suggested that keeping your phone close by can be a lifesaver.

It is beneficial to have important contact numbers, such as those of family members, friends, and emergency services, saved in your phone's contact list. This can save you valuable time in an emergency.

In today's world, our mobile phones have become an essential part of our lives. Make sure that your phone is always charged and within reach and consider keeping a backup battery or charger on hand.

Don't Let Accidents Climb Up on You

Climbing is a common activity that we all do at some point in our lives, whether it's to change a light bulb or retrieve something from a high shelf. To avoid accidents or injuries, it is important to approach climbing with caution and to take the necessary safety precautions.

Investing in a proper ladder is one of the most important climbing safety tips. Using a chair or other makeshift object to stand on can be hazardous and increases the risk of falling or getting injured. A sturdy ladder with slip-resistant feet can provide a stable base while also providing the necessary height to reach high places safely.

It is also important to be mindful of your surroundings when climbing. Never climb near an open window. A misstep can throw you off balance and out the window. Always leave enough space around you and keep any potential hazards, such as glassware or pointed objects, out of the way.

Finally, it is important to take your time when climbing and avoid rushing through the task. Climbing can be dangerous, and it is important to approach it with caution. Avoid climbing when you are not feeling well.

Securing Your Finance Privacy

Needless to say, it is obvious that women who live alone are usually financially secure and independent individuals who are able to look after ourselves. As a result, it is absolutely necessary for us to be cautious in order to shield ourselves from people who have malicious intentions.

Have you ever noticed how some people become more interested in your life when they learn about your financial situation? This is an unpleasant experience that many single women have encountered. As someone who has been set up with male friends as a potential partner from time to time, I've seen this firsthand. While some may be sincere, others may be attracted by the financial independence of a single woman. The last thing any of us wants is to be surrounded by people with bad intentions or fake friendships.

Remember that talking about money isn't the only way to let people know how you're doing financially. One can learn a lot about a person's financial situation by observing their job, home, and possessions. That's why it's so important to be cautious about who you share personal details with.

Remember that being financially independent is a source of pride, but it also presents unique challenges. As a woman living alone, it is crucial to protect yourself from those who may attempt to exploit your situation. You can maintain control of your life and surround yourself with people who care about you for who you are, not what you have, if you keep your financial information private.

Staying Safe During Power Outages

Power outages can occur anywhere in the world. It affects everyone, whether they live in the city or in the countryside. While some areas may be more prone to outages due to severe weather conditions, such as hurricanes or thunderstorms, power outages can also occur unexpectedly due to equipment failure or other issues. Power outages can affect both homes and businesses, and the duration of the outage varies depending on the cause and location. Some outages may last only a few minutes, while others may last hours or even days.

No matter where you live, it is always a good idea to be prepared for a power outage. This means making a plan and keeping important items on hand, like a torch or flashlight, batteries, a rechargeable backup battery, or, depending on where you live, even a generator. It is also critical to have a supply of non-perishable food and water on hand, as well as any medications that may be required.

Always keep your car's gas tank at least half full. If you are driving an electric car, that means you should not let your battery go flat before recharging.

Being prepared for a power outage can help you stay safe and comfortable during stressful situations, making you feel secure and in control. It only takes a few simple steps to prepare.

Your Daily Heartbeats

It is critical to maintain contact with friends and people you trust, especially if you live alone. A good way to accomplish this is to select a trusted friend and establish a routine of sending daily messages. You can pre-arrange with your friend that if you don't text each other on time, you will check in on each other. It's always a good idea to select someone you can rely on and who understands your situation.

I know how important this can be. I was suffering from a terrible migraine last Christmas and missed a message from my best friend wishing me a Merry Christmas. She noticed my lack of response and called me right away to check on me. It was a simple gesture, but it meant a lot to me.

This type of regular check-in can also help you and your friend maintain your mental health. Regardless of how strong you are, you may experience feelings of loneliness and isolation from time to time, especially when you are sick or during special occasions (for example, I was home alone last Christmas because I wasn't feeling well). It can make all the difference to have a friend who understands and cares. Furthermore, having someone to talk to about your day or the things that bother you is always beneficial.

The Distress Signal

The freedom of living alone can be liberating, but it also requires careful planning to avoid harm. You might call it paranoia but setting up a "distress signal" with someone you trust could save your life in an emergency.

Scammers can be found anywhere in the world and will try to take advantage of you if they can. Someone could pose as you and contact your loved ones, telling them you're in trouble and asking for financial assistance. That's why it's so crucial to develop a secret language with your closest confidants. Both three-word phrases, such as "I am dumb" or six-digit codes could do the job. You should only share this code with a close friend or a family member. In the event they receive a suspicious call and wonder if it's really you, they can simply ask for the code. You can rest assured that your friend or family member will understand that this is a serious call and that they should do what they can to assist you.

Make sure that only you and your trusted friend or family member know about this code. This way, if they receive a call that seems suspicious, they can ask for the code to confirm it's really you. Your friend or family member will appreciate that this is a genuine call, and that they need to take action to help you.

Additionally, this code can also be used as a distress signal. If you find yourself in a dangerous situation and cannot communicate directly, you can use the code to alert your friend or family member that you need help.

Taking the time to establish a distress signal with someone you trust can give you peace of mind and help keep you safe in potentially dangerous situations. So, choose someone you trust, create a code, and stay safe.

Chapter One (Day 1) Summary

In this chapter, we've talked about the importance of being prepared for emergencies and how to keep ourselves safe and secure at home. From having a well-stocked first aid kit and medicines to securing our doors and locks, we've covered a lot of ground. We've also discussed that it is important to stay connected with someone you trust . As we move on to chapter two, we'll explore some useful household hacks that can make our daily lives easier and more efficient. These simple tips and tricks can help us troubleshoot common problems and handle day-to-day challenges with ease.

Chapter Two

MASTERING HOUSEHOLD HACKS

"If you want something you've never had, you must be willing to do something you've never done."

Thomas Jefferson

Have you ever been caught in an unexpected household issue, such as a clogged sink or a malfunctioning WiFi connection? I used to feel frustrated and helpless, but instead of waiting around for a handyman to come to the rescue, I decided to take matters into my own hands and equip myself with some simple hacks and troubleshooting skills. And now, I'm sharing my secrets with you in this chapter! So say goodbye to the frustration and hello to a new sense of empowerment. Get ready to handle unexpected situations with confidence and a little bit of humor (because let's face it, sometimes you just have to laugh at the absurdity of it all).

It is important to note that while I am sharing these hacks and tips with you, I am not a professional or trained electrician or plumber. The purpose of this chapter is to empower you with the knowledge to confidently tackle some household issues on your own, but it is also important to know when to seek professional help. If a problem seems too complex or dangerous, do not hesitate to call in the experts. However, for small issues that you can safely troubleshoot and fix yourself, these tips can save you time, money, and the hassle of waiting for a service call. So, let's get started and equip ourselves with the skills to handle unexpected situations in our homes.

Troubleshoot Wi-Fi Problems

In troubleshooting Wi-Fi problems, it's important to isolate the source of the issue, whether it's the Wi-Fi modem, the computer or mobile device, or ONT if you're using fiber (Optical Network Terminal). The ONT is a device that converts optical signals to electrical signals and vice versa, allowing for communication between the optical fiber cable and other network devices. It's provided by your Internet service provider and is installed near your Wi-Fi modem.

First, check whether both your computer and mobile device

are picking up the Wi-Fi signal (that the signal icon has bars). If only one of your devices is picking up the signal while the other does not, it is likely that it is a device connection problem. Reboot the device that has no signal.

If you only have one device, or if both your computer and mobile device have Wi-Fi signal but you cannot connect to the Internet, it is likely that either your Wi-Fi modem or the ONT, or both have problems. Go to the next step.

Check the power and status lights on the ONT to make sure they're lit. If they're not, or if you see a red light, the ONT may not be receiving power or may be malfunctioning. In this case, try unplugging the ONT from its power source and plugging it back in after a minute or so. This can help reset the device and clear any errors that may be causing the problem.

If the power and status lights on the ONT are both illuminated without any red light, the issue may be with your Wi-Fi modem. In this case, try reset the Wi-Fi modem (power off and then power on).

If you fail to connect to the Internet after all attempts, try contacting your Internet service provider for assistance. There may be a network outage, or they may need to send a technician to your home to diagnose and fix the problem.

In addition to these troubleshooting steps, there are a few things you can do to help prevent Wi-Fi issues in the first place. For example, make sure your Wi-Fi modem is in a central location in your home and not obstructed by walls or furniture. This can help ensure a strong and stable Wi-Fi signal throughout your home.

Understand Your Circuit Breaker Panel

The circuit breaker panel (a.k.a. breaker box) is one of the most important components of your home's electrical system, yet many people don't know where it is or how to use it. As you're living alone, it is essential to be familiar with the breaker box.

The first step is to locate the breaker box in your home. It's usually found in the basement, garage, or utility room, and it contains all of the fuses or circuit breakers for your home's electrical system. Take the time to familiarize yourself with the layout of the box, including the labels and markings for each switch or fuse. I keep a photo of the box on my phone.

During a power outage, it is important to check if the entire house or just part of it lost power. If the entire house lost power, see if your neighbors still have power. If your immediate neighbors still have power, it is likely that the issue is with your home's electrical system. This is the time when you need to go to the breaker box.

First, check the breaker box to see if any of the switches have tripped. A tripped switch will be in the "off" position, whereas a working switch will be in the "on" position. Simply flip the switch back to the "on" position to restore power to that part of your home. I once paid $100 for a call-out and all the electrician did was flip a switch. He completed the job in less than two minutes.

It is important to note that if you are unsure or uncomfortable about how to safely operate the breaker box, you should contact a licensed electrician. Working with electricity can be dangerous, so it is always better to err on the safe side.

In addition to restoring power during an outage, the breaker box can also help you identify and resolve electrical issues in your home. For example, if you notice that certain appliances or a particular power outlet is not working, you can use the breaker box to determine if a circuit breaker has tripped or if a fuse has blown.

In some cases, a fuse may need to be replaced entirely. Please contact a professional electrician for help.

In conclusion, knowing the location and operation of the breaker box is crucial for homeowners. By taking the time to familiarize yourself with the breaker box and its components, you'll be better equipped to handle some unexpected electrical issues that may arise.

Locate the Water Shut Off Valve

Knowing the location of your home's main water shut-off valve is just as important as knowing where your breaker box is located. The main water shut-off valve is often located near the water meter, but it can also be located elsewhere, such as near the street, inside the home, or in a basement or crawl space.

You also need to know the water meter, which is a device the water company measures your water usage. It is typically located near the street or close to the edge of your property line. If you live in an apartment, the water meter is typically located in a utility closet or a mechanical room. If you're unsure about where it is, ask your building management or landlord.

In the event of a plumbing emergency, it's important to act

fast and turn off the main water shut-off valve before calling a plumber. This can prevent further water damage to your home and your other possessions. Additionally, it's always a good idea to have the contact information of a reliable plumber on hand in case of an emergency.

Resolve an Unusual Water Bill

Have you ever opened your water bill and been surprised by how much you need to pay? If this is the case, don't worry; there are some simple steps you can take to find out if there is a problem.

To begin, turn off all of your appliances, such as the washing machine and dishwasher, etc. Then check and make sure no taps in your home is running. Check your water meter to see if the reading dial is still moving. If the reading continues to move even when no water is being used, there is most likely a leak somewhere in your pipes.

If you suspect a leak, you must act quickly to avoid further damage and additional costs. A leak can cause mold growth, water damage to your property, and even an increase in your water bill.

If you happen to live in a rental property and discover a leak, don't hesitate to contact your landlord as soon as possible! But if you own your own sweet abode, it's a good idea to call in and get a pro plumber to check things out and find the source of the issue. Unless you're a DIY plumbing wizard (which is highly unlikely), don't try to fix it yourself or you might end up with an even bigger headache. Trust me, I learned that the hard way!

Other than checking for leaks, there are other things you can do to reduce your water bill. Install low-flow showerheads and faucets, repair any dripping faucets, and only run your dishwasher and washing machine when they are full.

By taking these steps, you can save money on your water bill while also ensuring that your plumbing system is working properly. Remember that if you suspect a leak, you should address it as soon as possible to avoid further damage and expenses.

Jump Start a Car

Keeping a jumper cable in your car is always a good idea, but what if you get stranded somewhere and there is no other vehicle nearby to jump start you? Portable cell batteries come in handy in this situation. I am referring to the portable battery jump-starter kit. It is similar to those portable mobile phone chargers. It can jump start a car even if you don't have access to another vehicle.

Having a portable battery jump-starter can save you from having to wait for someone else's help. Whether you're in a remote location, a busy parking lot, or parking in a position that makes it difficult for another vehicle to come close to you, having a portable battery jump-starter will give you peace of mind, knowing that you don't need to worry if your car's battery suddenly gives up on you, which is definitely one for the embarrassing hall of fame.

Portable battery jump-starters are compact and lightweight, which can easily fit in the trunk or even the glove box. They are easy to use too. Make sure you connect the positive and negative terminals correctly. Most models come with clear instructions, and you don't need any special skills or training to use them.

Many portable battery jump-starters come with extra features, like built-in flashlights, USB charging ports, and air compressors for inflating flat tires. Personally, I've found the tire inflating function to be the most helpful of all these handy extras.

I highly recommend keeping a portable battery jump-starter in your car, but there's one thing you need to remember - make sure to recharge the battery every once in a while as the battery will drain even when not in use! The last thing you want is to be stuck with a dead car battery and a useless jump-starter.

Unclog a Drain or the Sink

Okay, it's time for some dirty work. Let's get started on learning how to unclog a blocked sink or drainage. Trust me, it's not as frightening as it sounds!

To start, it is important to comprehend what causes blockages. Typically, it is caused by a buildup of grease, food particles, hair, or soap scum. To avoid drain blockages, avoid pouring grease or oil down the drain, use a drain catcher to catch food particles and hair. But despite all the prevention measures, sinks get clogged from time to time. if your sink or drainage becomes clogged, don't panic! Most of the time you can unclog it yourself. A plunger is the first tool you'll need. Yes, you read that correctly: the plunger used to unclog your toilet can also be used to unclog your sink or drainage, but you may not want to use the same one for your kitchen sink.

To use the plunger, first make sure there is enough water in the sink or drain to cover the plunger's bottom. Then, place the plunger over the drain and begin plunging up and down to create a vacuum that will force the blockage out.

If the plunger doesn't work, you can try using a drain snake. A drain snake is a long, flexible wire with a hook at the end. Insert the wire down the drain and twist it around, trying to hook onto the blockage and pull it out.

Baking soda and vinegar are another alternative. Pour a cup of baking soda and a cup of vinegar down the drain. Cover the drain and set aside for at least 30 minutes. Then, pour boiling water down the drain to clear the obstruction.

If everything else fails, it's time to call in the experts. If you can't fix the problem yourself, don't be afraid to call a plumber. It's better to fix it now rather than later, before it becomes a bigger, more expensive problem.

So there you have it! Unclogging a blocked sink or drainage is not as scary as it seems. Keep a plunger or drain snake handy and try to resolve the problem. And if all else fails, just call a plumber with a smile on your face!

Maintain a Handyman List

When it comes to home maintenance, it's almost inevitable that you'll need the help of a handyman or tradesman at some point. From minor repairs to major renovations, it is critical to have a list of reliable contacts on hand. Here are some of the reasons why such a list is essential.

Keeping a list of reliable handymen on hand can save you a lot of trouble. You don't want to go on a search when your shower only gives you cold water and your shampoo is still on your hair. But with a pre-vetted list of professionals, you can skip the search and get the assistance you require quickly.

Second, keeping a list of reliable handymen or tradesmen allows you to get to know them better over time. You can build rapport and trust when you use them regularly. This can result in better service and faster response times.

Thirdly, having a list of reliable handymen or tradesmen means you can be sure their advice is trustworthy. This can give you peace of mind that the issue will be resolved properly. But don't always blindly trust their advice. You still need to make judgement call and compare quotes especially for big jobs.

Start by asking friends, family, and neighbors for suggestions of trustworthy contractors. Word of mouth is a great way to find reliable people in your area. You can also search online for reviews and ratings of local handymen or tradesmen. Make sure to read reviews from multiple sources to get a well-rounded understanding of their reputation.

Building a list of reliable handymen might seem like a tedious task, but trust me, it's worth it. When the going gets tough and things break down, you'll be sitting pretty with the peace of mind that you've got some top-notch tradespeople on speed dial. Who doesn't want a little peace and quiet during hectic moments!

Learn Some First Aid Skills

Living alone is liberating, but don't forget that you promised to take full responsibility for your own safety and well-being. Learning basic first-aid techniques is one way to accomplish this. It is critical for a woman living alone to be prepared for unexpected injuries or emergencies.

One of the most important first aid techniques to learn is how to apply direct pressure to a wound to stop bleeding. This can be as simple as using a clean cloth or bandage and applying pressure to the wound until the bleeding stops. It's also important to elevate the injured area above the level of the heart to help reduce bleeding.

In addition to stopping bleeding, knowing how to properly use a cold and hot compress. If you have a small injury like a sprain or a bruise, putting a cold compress on it can help reduce the pain and swelling. When the swelling has gone down, on the other hand, applying heat can help the wound heal faster.

If you suspect a more serious injury, such as a fracture or dislocation, it's important not to try to move the affected area. Instead, call for assistance and wait for help to arrive. In the meantime, keep the affected area as still as possible.

By learning these simple first-aid techniques, you can feel more at ease knowing you're ready to handle some minor injuries or emergencies that may come up. It's always a good idea to keep a first aid kit at home. Remember, taking care of ourselves is the ultimate form of self-love! So, let's equip ourselves with the knowledge and skills we need to handle any situation that comes our way. With some basic first aid techniques in our back pockets, we can feel confident and capable no matter what life throws our way. And who knows? You might just impress yourself with how much of a superhero you could be.

Upkeep Home Appliances

Are you tired of your appliances breaking down right when you need them the most? I have some tips to help you keep your appliances in tip-top shape!

Let's start with our kitchen appliances, starting with the in-sink garbage disposer. The key to keeping it in good shape is to avoid throwing bones or hard objects into it, as this can damage the blades. Last week was quite an eventful one for my friend. She called a plumber to fix her garbage disposer and, wouldn't you know it, I was at her home when that happened. You'll never believe what the plumber found in there - chipped china pieces & a screw!"

Another important tip is to make sure you don't accidentally drop any cutlery into the disposer, as this can also cause damage. To clean the garbage disposer, you can use a mixture of ice and vinegar to freshen it up and remove any buildup. Simply pour the mixture into the disposal and turn it on. Finally, make sure to run water for a few seconds after using the garbage disposer to flush out any remaining debris. Follow these tips and your in-sink garbage disposer will stay in tip-top shape for years to come!

Another important tip is, always read the manual that comes with your appliance. I know, I know, manuals can be tedious and boring, but they contain valuable information on how to use and maintain your appliance properly. Trust me, just like this book, it's worth the read!

Secondly, always clean your appliances regularly. For example, your dishwasher might look clean, but over time it can accumulate dirt and grime that can affect its performance. A quick wipe down with a sponge or cloth can do wonders for your appliance's longevity.

Next up, check the filters in your appliances. Many appliances, such as air conditioners and vacuum cleaners, have filters that need to be cleaned or replaced regularly. Clogged filters can lead to poor performance, increased energy consumption, and even damage to the appliance.

Lastly, be mindful of how you use your appliances. For example, overloading your washing machine can cause it to break down, and using harsh chemicals can damage your dishwasher. Always use your appliances according to the instructions in the manual.

Remember, taking care of your appliances can save you money in the long run. So, let's show those appliances some care and love, and keep them humming along smoothly!

Change a Tire

Alright girls, after so many pages, I already consider you as a friend, and I have a confession to make - I have never changed a tire in my life! Sure, I've watched a bunch of online videos and know the theory of it, but when it comes to putting it into practice... let's just say I'm not quite there yet. But fear not, my dear friends! I have a proposition for you - let's have a contest! The challenge is simple - write an article teaching others how to change a tire using only words. That's right, no pictures, no videos, just good old-fashioned words. The winner will receive... well, the satisfaction of knowing you helped your fellow humans, and maybe a virtual high-five from me. So, what do you say? Are you up for the challenge?

Raid Of Bugs

As much as I hate to talk about it, let's discuss the raid of bugs. Whether you live in a house or an apartment, insects always seem to find their way in. One common problem is ants, especially when you have pets that leave food in their bowls. To prevent ants from invading your home, try placing your pet's food bowl inside a larger bowl filled with water. This way, the ants won't be able to access the food and won't be drawn to your home.

If you already have an ant problem, don't fret! There are effective solutions you can try, such as ant powder and ant baits. Ant powder is a fine powder form of insecticide that kills ants on contact, making it easy to wipe away the affected area. However, it's important to remember that this is only a temporary solution.

To really tackle the problem, find the "path" that the ants are taking and place ant baits along the way. Ant baits work by attracting the ants with a sugary or protein-based substance, which they then bring back to their colony to share with the others. This method may take a few days to work, but it's a more permanent solution as it eliminates the entire ant colony.

In addition to ants, there are other common household bugs that can be a nuisance, such as roaches and spiders. To prevent these pests from taking over your home, keep your living space clean and tidy. Make sure to regularly take out the trash and keep food stored in sealed containers. If you do have a pest problem, don't hesitate to call a professional pest control service to handle the situation. You only need to do this once in a while.

Another useful tool in preventing bug invasions is caulking. Check your home for any gaps or cracks in the walls, baseboards, or windows. Use caulking to seal up any openings where bugs might be able to sneak in.

Let's face it, bugs are like that one neighbor who always overstays their welcome - annoying and persistent. But fear not, my friend! With some clever tricks and a bit of bug-proofing, you can make your home a bug-free oasis. So the next time you spot an army of ants raiding your kitchen, don't panic - just take a deep breath, grab the ant powder, and show those six-legged invaders who's boss!

Chapter Two (Day 2) Summary

In this chapter, we've covered some clever household hacks that will help you tackle day-to-day challenges with ease. From troubleshooting your Wi-Fi connection to fixing a clogged drain, these tips will save you time, money, and frustration. We hope you've found them helpful!

As important as it is to stay on top of household tasks, it's equally important to build good financial habits that will set you up for a stable and secure future. In the next chapter, we'll explore some key strategies for managing your money wisely and achieving your financial goals. So, let's dive in!

Chapter Three

BUILDING GOOD FINANCIAL HABITS

"It's not your salary that makes you rich, it's your spending habits."

Charles A. Jaffe

As an independent woman living alone, it's essential to have a solid money management mindset. Chapter Three guides you in building healthy financial habits and achieving financial stability. We all know that managing finances can be tough when you don't have someone to share the household expenses, so the first step is to get a handle on your income and expenses, and that's what this chapter is all about.

We will explore ways to examine your finances and gain a clear understanding of your current situation. Afterwards, we will learn techniques to keep track of the cashflow and design a plan tailored to your needs. In this chapter, I will introduce a financial health check and share some useful tools with you as well. Trust me, every stage of life brings different financial challenges, but with some knowledge and self-discipline, you can build a sustainable plan and lifestyle. Let's get started!

Build Financial Stability for a Lifetime

Living alone can be a liberating experience, but it doesn't mean one is exempt from financial obligations. We all face unique challenges at different life stages. Whether you're in your twenties, thirties, forties, fifties, or beyond, it's important to manage your finances carefully and plan for the future.

For those in their twenties, starting a career can be an exciting time. You may be earning your own money for the first time and have the urge to purchase the things you've always wanted. However, it is important to remember that being a young worker usually means earning less than one's senior counterparts. Thus, managing finances cautiously and avoiding overspending is crucial at this stage of life.

In your thirties, you may be looking to save up for a down payment on a home or plan a well-deserved vacation. While you may be earning more money than in your twenties, it's important to make a plan and set financial goals.

As you enter your forties, you may face additional obligations, such as supporting children with a single income after a divorce or the loss of a partner. Even if you don't have children to support, retirement planning may start to become a priority. It is important to assess your finances and plan for your future.

When you reach your fifties, retirement may be on the horizon, and you may start worrying about how you'll fund your retirement years. It's important to plan ahead and make sure you have enough saving to keep you live comfortably.

As you enter your sixties and beyond, it is important to set aside funds for medical expenses. Healthcare costs can be a significant financial burden, especially as one ages.

At all stages of life, it is important to plan one's finances carefully, especially when living alone. It can be overwhelming to consider all the financial responsibilities you have, but don't worry; there are resources available to help you. Keep reading, and together we can create a plan to give you peace of mind and financial security.

Calculate Disposable Income

Most people do not understand the concept of disposable income and discretionary spending. Let us clear this up before moving on. Disposable income is the amount of money a person or household has after paying taxes and essential expenses, such as housing, food, transportation, and other necessary living costs. Discretionary spending refers to the money that remains after essential expenses have been paid and can be used for non-essential items or services, such as dining out, entertainment, or vacations. In other words, discretionary spending is a subset of disposable income.

To understand your financial well-being, the first step is to determine your disposable income. Grab a notebook or create a spreadsheet to list your financial obligations, such as quarterly or annual payments, including life insurance, health insurance, car insurance, school fees for your children (if applicable), etc.

After you have all your obligations listed out, divide those annual amounts by 12 to determine how much you should set aside each month for each responsibility. For example, if the annual life insurance is $1,200, put down $100 per month. I've created a set of spreadsheets for those who are tech-savvy. You may print them out if you prefer the classic pen-and-paper approach. Please find the download instructions on page 7.

Next, list out all your monthly bills, including your mortgage or rent payment, utilities, phone and Internet bills, and any subscription services you have, such as cloud storage and video-on-demand service. Again, write down the amount for each expense on a monthly basis. Double check to make sure you have all of them covered.

Now it is time to add up the two categories of expenses to determine your total monthly obligation. Make sure to include everything, no matter how insignificant the expense may seem. Once you have calculated your total monthly expenses, subtract this amount from your monthly income after taxes. The remaining amount is your monthly disposable income. Wait a minute! This is not the amount that can be spent on discretionary spending yet. Please keep reading.

Build a Reserve

It's important to keep in mind that unexpected expenses, such as car repairs or medical bills, can arise at any time. It's a good idea to build up an emergency fund to cover such expenses. Ideally, you should set aside enough to cover at least three to six months of your living expenses. This is a cushion for you to fall back on in case of unexpected situations.

At this point, it's time to give your finances a health check. It's simple and should not take long. First, count all assets that you can easily convert into cash. This includes money in a bank account and shares in listed companies. Add up the total and see if it's equal to or greater than three months' worth of your living expenses. If you want to be on the safe side, shoot for six months' worth of reserve. Having at least three months' worth of reserves will give you peace of mind in case of an unexpected job loss. If your reserve is smaller than three months, work hard to accumulate it. With some commitment and self-control, this is easier than you think.

Remember, it is always wise to be on the safe side. Remember my friend Athena who I mentioned in Chapter One? She is a good role module who built a solid reserve for rainy days. When Athena unexpectedly found herself out of a job, she was able to enjoy her six months downtime without constantly worrying about her finances. She even treated herself to a trip to Paris, because why not? Having a reserve not only gives you a sense of security and peace of mind, but it also allows you to take advantage of opportunities that come your way. So, instead of feeling like you're constantly treading water, why not start building up that reserve now?

Talking about building up a reserve, I suggest keeping a separate bank account dedicated to this purpose. To me, I've found this practice effective. This allows me to keep track of my savings clearly and prevent them from getting mixed up with other funds. You may also consider establishing a regular deposit routine, such as setting up automatic transfers after each payday or transferring leftover funds at the end of the month. By doing so, you are developing a good habit in pursuing your financial goals.

Let's face it, emergencies happen, whether it's a sudden job loss or your car and computer deciding to go on strike at the same time. It's important to build up a reserve of spare cash; think of it as a sacred sword that you only draw when it is most needed. Make it a habit to put some of your hard-earned cash into this emergency fund each month. The amount you set aside should be appropriate - not too much, not too little. Set a realistic goal that won't leave you living off bread and tap water. Trust me, your future self will thank you for being a financial superhero.

Keep Track of Monthly Spending

Keeping track of your daily spending is a habit that has served me well for over twenty years. Yes, you read that right! I use a professional accounting package to record all my daily expenses, and I truly believe that the effort has paid off. With this habit, I have built up the confidence to always know how much money I have in reserve, what my outstanding balance is on my home mortgage, my total credit card outstanding, and how much I spend on average, on what area, every month.

You may not need a professional accounting software. Simply use computer spreadsheets or even pen and paper is good enough. I highly recommend this practice as it allows you in gaining a better understanding of your financial situation and feel more in control of your money.

Eleanor is a close friend who I catch up regularly. She is a carefree person who doesn't like rules or constraints. When I first talked about my daily bookkeeping habit, Eleanor was astonished and thought I was overly complicating things.

Until one day, Eleanor turned to me for advice for an accounting software for her new start-up. I shared with her my experience and explained to her how to set that up. Out of curiosity, Eleanor started using the software for her personal finance. Two months later, Eleanor shared with me her excitement. Eleanor was amazed that understanding her assets, debts, cash on hand and monthly expenses gives her new insights of her financial situation, which subsequently strengthens her confidence in making important financial decisions.

Another benefit of keeping track of your monthly expense is to develop an understanding of your spending pattern. For example, I once discovered that I have been spending far too much on skincare and cosmetics. I consciously made adjustment before the situation goes out of control.

In the bonus download, I share with you a spreadsheet that I use to track my daily expenses. I suggest you download and start tracking your monthly discretionary spending. Set a limit for yourself and track your spending, so that you can make sure you're not spending more than you can afford.

This also allows you to identify areas of potential overspending and where you can cut back. By doing that, you can make adjustments before things go out of control.

I suggest that you begin by tracking your expenses for three consecutive months. This allows you to gain a deeper understanding of your spending patterns, the categories that account for the majority of your spending, and whether or not this makes sense. I assure you that you will acquire new perspectives on your own financial well-being. After three months, you can choose whether to continue doing so regularly or to conduct periodic financial health assessments.

Manage Your Spending

Overspending must be avoided in order to maintain financial stability and a sense of security. Overspending can cause not only financial problems, but also feelings of guilt and stress. Living within your means and being conscious of your spending habits can assist you in avoiding these negative emotions and leading a more fulfilling life.

The most common way of overspending is through impulse purchases. When Patricia called me and cried out for help for the third time, I knew this was serious and her problems must be fixed. Patricia could only afford minimum payments for her credit cards, and her home was packed with new items and some unopened shopping bags. Patricia used to use window shopping as a form of entertainment, especially when she was stressed or wanted to escape from a problem.

In the next section, I will talk about why we should avoid going shopping when we are emotionally weak. It is a bad idea to go shopping when you are stressed or hungry. I will elaborate further.

Talking about shopping habits, it's easy to get caught up in the moment and overspend, especially when we see something we really want. However, it is critical to exercise self-control and avoid overspending, especially when you come across sales and other promotional activities. While these can seem like great opportunities to save money, they can also be a trap if you're not careful. Stick to your budget and avoid making purchases just because they're on sale. Remember, if you don't need it, it's not a good deal no matter how much you save. Remember, two hundred dollars in cash is worth far more than a pair of shoes that cost you $200.

Below is a summary of strategies for prevention of overspending:
- Always have a budget and stick to it.
- Track your spending and review it regularly.
- Avoid impulse purchases.
- Wait for a few days before making big purchases to ensure you really need them.
- Develop a shopping list before shopping.
- Stick to your shopping list and avoid adding extra items.
- Minimize the use of credit cards for non-essential purchases.
- Avoid shopping when you are hungry or tired, as this can lead to impulse buys.
- Limit your exposure to advertisements and

marketing campaigns (why put yourself in front of temptations!).
- Avoid comparing yourself to others and trying to keep up with their spending habits.
- Consider the long-term value of a purchase, not just the short-term satisfaction.
- Avoid shopping as a form of entertainment.
- Set financial goals and work towards them.
- Find free or low-cost activities for entertainment.
- Avoid shopping online when feeling bored or stressed.
- Be mindful of sales and discounts, and only buy what you really need, not what you want!
- Avoid subscribing to unnecessary services or memberships. They add up significantly.
- Use cash for discretionary spending and limit the amount you carry. Sometimes I simply keep my credit cards at home.
- Reward yourself for achieving financial goals with non-financial or low value rewards, such as a book or a bottle of wine.

You can build a better financial future for yourself by exercising self-control and avoiding overspending. This means more emergency savings, more money for long-term goals, and less stress when it comes to adverse moments.

Stay Away from Window Shopping

You may be tempted to go window shopping when you are anxious or stressed. This is especially easy if you live in a city or near a mall. Watch out! It can be a slippery slope into impulse purchase, which can lead to overspending.

We are human. We have emotions and cannot remain strong and rational all the time. When we are stressed, it is natural to seek ways to find comfort so as to make ourselves feel better. Purchasing something can provide us with that instant gratification and a sense of satisfaction, which in turn leads to a temporary relief.

Window shopping is a popular form of entertainment for

people who live in urban regions with high concentrations of malls and boutiques. This is because it is a simple method to kill time and that the sights and noises of a crowded shopping area can be stimulating. However, the sales promotions, ambient setting, background music, and commercials are made to entice you into purchasing goods that you do not need.

Window shopping may seem harmless, but it can quickly turn into actual shopping and before you know it. You might be making purchases that you cannot afford. While it may provide a temporary relief from stress or anxiety, the long-term consequences of financial difficulties can lead to an overwhelming sense of despair. So, it's important to be mindful of our spending habits and avoid using shopping as a form of emotional relief.

Furthermore, window shopping can be a form of social pressure, as we may feel compelled to keep up with our friends or peers who are always buying the latest fashion or technology. We may worry that we will be left behind or be seen as uncool if we don't have the latest gadgets or designer clothes. This pressure is especially strong for younger people who are still forming their identities and trying to fit in with their peer group.

In conclusion, while it may seem harmless to use window shopping as a form of entertainment, it can quickly lead to impulse purchase and overspending.

Going back to Patricia, I sat down with her and examined her financial situation. I gave her my suggestions—those that you have read earlier in this book. It was found out that she was spending more than she could afford. Her monthly expenses were greater than her disposal income. I explained to Patricia that she needs to start living within her means and plan to pay off her debt. Patricia took my advice. She found a part-time job to increase her income and made more than the minimum payment on her credit cards, prioritizing the card with the highest interest rate first. She started tracking her monthly spending and created a budget, which helped her identify areas where she could cut back. It wasn't easy, but with time, she was able to pay off her debt and regained control of her finances.

Watch Out for Online Shopping

Online shopping has the potential to become a trap that draws you into an endless stream of alluring goods. It is simple to add products to your shopping cart and check out without even noticing how much you've spent. I suggest you set up a budget in advance and restrict yourself from overspending. For me, I set aside a monthly budget dedicated for online purchase. It is almost guaranteed that aimlessly browsing an online marketplace will result in purchasing extra items that you hadn't planned to buy. This is because online shopping itself is a fun and rewarding experience.

In recent years, online shopping has become increasingly important to our daily lives. Online shopping has become more popular because of its convenience and usually lower prices. However, we must be wary of the temptation to go overboard when shopping online due to the ease it provides.

First and foremost, we need to consider shipping costs. It's important to factor in the shipping cost when making a purchase decision, especially when shopping from international websites. Sometimes the shipping cost may outweigh the cost of the product itself, making it not worth the purchase. What you need to consider is the total cost of ownership, not just the product price. Also, product warranty and maintenance are all major considerations when buying electronic products from overseas platforms.

Another risk of online shopping is the tendency to buy extra items that are not needed. The ease of shopping online may lead us to buy things that we wouldn't have considered if we were shopping in a physical store. The ease of electronic payment lessens our sense of the value of money, as opposed to when we physically exchange cash or use a credit card in-store. It's important to be mindful and focus on what you need instead of what you want.

Online shopping platforms are designed to entice us to buy more. Yes, that's all businesses do, whether online or offline, right? But there is something powerful about technology. They track our shopping preferences and browsing history and use this information to push targeted ads to us. This can be a trap, as it exposes us to temptations and may result in impulse purchases.

It's important to be aware of the cost and benefits of online shopping and to truly enjoy the experience. Remember, you need to be in control instead of being controlled. As mentioned earlier, it is useful to set a budget for online shopping and stick to it. Another tip is to avoid engaging in shopping behavior when you're feeling emotional or stressed, including browsing online marketplaces. When one is emotional despair, it is easy to buy impulsively because your brain will entice you in doing something to feel good. It's important to shop with a clear and rational state of mind.

I must admit, I'm a big fan of online shopping. When I shop online, I feel like going on an adventure. Discovering new things and trying them out is an enjoyable experience. Like all of you, I've had a few missteps, like buying bad quality garments that look nothing like the photos on the website, and some chalk-like eyeshadow that went straight in the trash. Overall, my online shopping experiences have been great. I always stick to my rules that I shared with you above. I reckon self-control is the secret key and with some basic principles in mind, one would not get carried away with the convenience of online shopping. By setting a budget and sticking to it, you can have a fun and exciting shopping experience too.

Be Mindful on Monthly Subscriptions

Have you ever added up your monthly subscriptions and found out how much they cost you in total every month?

One of the subjects I talk about frequently with friends is monthly subscriptions. I recently challenged my friends to take stock of their monthly subscriptions. The results were eye-opening. Some were shocked to find out that they spend over $100 per month on various services like cloud storage, productivity software, music streaming, and video on demand, etc. Even more surprising, some of my friends even discovered that they were still paying for apps they are no longer using. It served as a wake-up call to us. We want to give someone our hard-earned money in exchange for something of worth, right? This demonstrates the need to keep track of our spending, especially when it comes to monthly subscriptions.

While it may appear to be a few dollars here and there, those monthly charges can build up and become a significant amount that could affect your financial healthiness.

Monthly subscriptions is likely one of the most common pitfalls we face in today's world. It's easy to forget about a subscription after you set that up, and leaving your credit card details on file may result in future deductions that you may not even be aware of. Both my mom and I have experienced credit card deductions for a service that was meant to be a one-off payment. I had to call the credit card company to file a dispute. I eventually got my money back, but no one could compensate me for the trouble and frustration I had gone through.

It's easy to forget to cancel a subscription even if you're no longer using the app or service. Therefore, it is useful to maintain a running list of your monthly subscriptions. You should also examine your phone's subscription list regularly. Conduct housekeeping from time to time and unsubscribe from apps and services that are no longer required. Also, it may be useful to set notifications to remind yourself about "free trial plans" and "annual renewal" that have your credit card information on file, in case you may forget to terminate them before the trial period expires.

To summarize, it is impossible to completely stay away from monthly subscriptions, therefore it is important to be cautious and keep track of your expenses.

Manage Credit Card Spendings

When I was in my twenties and got my first credit card, I was thrilled by the idea of having a piece of plastic that allowed me to make purchases so conveniently. It was almost addictive when I found out I can own things without even having sufficient funds on hand. Soon I saw advertisements for interest-free financing plans on big-ticket items like furniture and electronics. I jumped at the opportunity to get those items. I thought I was getting good deals.

I soon got to know that those interest-free financing plans brought me more trouble than they were beneficial. It was true that I wasn't paying interest, but the monthly payments quickly added up, which was so significant that it took up a large share of my monthly earnings. I found myself struggling to keep up. The real trouble started when I went on an overseas trip and forgot to make one of my credit card payments on time. When I returned home, I found out that I had been charged a hefty late fee and my interest rate had skyrocketed. I was shocked and frustrated that I had to pay so much money just for forgetting one payment.

That experience taught me a valuable lesson about the importance of being responsible with credit. While interest-free financing plans can seem like a good idea at the moment, they can quickly become a burden if not managed properly. I learned to be more mindful of my credit card spending and to always make my payments on time to avoid penalties and fees.

Now, as a more experienced credit card user, I am more careful about the financing plans I choose and make sure to read the terms and conditions carefully. I also make sure to always pay my credit card balance in full and on time to avoid any unnecessary fees and interest charges. It's a lesson I learned the hard way, but one that has helped me become a more responsible and savvy credit card user.

Settle Debts and Repayment Promptly

Talking about credit card late payment, it is necessary to understand why we should always pay our debts on time. I know it's not the most glamorous topic, but trust me, it's essential for a happy and stress-free life in the long run.

First of all, let's talk about those pesky late fees. You know what I'm talking about - that little charge that seems trivial, but adds up to a big dent in your wallet over time. It is unwise to throw our hard-earned money away on something which is in fact avoidable.

And don't even get me started on the penalty interest charges! Those can really sneak up on us if we're not careful. Before you know it, you're paying more in interest than you ever did for the original purchase. It's like a never-ending cycle of debt that's hard to get out of.

The stress that comes with debt is bothersome. I know some of you might have been there - lying awake at night, worrying about how you're going to make that next payment. It's not a fun feeling, and it can really take a toll on our mental and physical health. Plus, when we're stressed about money, it's easy to make impulsive decisions that we'll regret later.

Furthermore, if you default on a payment or miss a payment deadline, it can negatively impact your credit score and make it more difficult to secure a loan in the future. You may also end up paying higher interest rates or additional fees as a result.

So, what's the solution? It's simple - pay your debts on time. Set up automatic payments so you don't even have to think about it. And if you're feeling overwhelmed by your debts, talk to a financial advisor or credit counselor. They can help you come up with a plan to get back on track.

Remember my dear friends. Don't let debt and finance stress you out. With a little planning and discipline, we can take control of our finances and live a great life.

Set Realistic Financial Goals

Did you know that human brains are wired to pursue happiness? It is what keeps us going every day. We all want to live happily. That's why building a strong financial reserve is important. Financial security and stability could lead to long-term happiness. But keep in mind that long-term happiness should not be at the expense of short-term sadness. In other words, we must not make the current "you" feel miserable. I don't want you to suppress your needs too much, only to end up giving in to a surge of 'revenge shopping' later.

Setting realistic financial goals is important. If you set goals that are unattainable, you will live a very lean budget and you will feel that you are suffering. No one wants to suffer, and your mental strength will gradually drain over time. It only requires a small trigger for you to give up. You will suddenly find yourself engage in a shopping surge, which is what I referred to as "revenge shopping".

However, after the shopping craze, you are likely to feel bad and your mental state will fluctuate again. You feel bad because your shopping surge brought you further away from your financial goals. You'll then feel guilty for overspending.

The vicious cycle will continue. Some people will even punish themselves and set even tighter budgets, hoping to make up for the extra spending. That vicious cycle will not be broken, until one day one finally gives up and thinks that the method does not work for her.

The key to setting realistic financial goals is to give yourself enough gratification, in other words, allow yourself some dopamine. Dopamine is the chemical in our brain that makes us feel happy and satisfied. When we achieve a goal, our brain releases dopamine, which makes us feel good. That's why it's important to set small, achievable goals. When you achieve these goals, your brain will release dopamine, and you'll feel good about yourself.

For example, if you're trying to save money, set a goal to save a small amount each week. Maybe it's $20, maybe it's $50, whatever is realistic for you. When you achieve that goal, celebrate it! Treat yourself to a small reward, like a fancy coffee or a new book. This will help your brain release dopamine and make you feel good about your progress.

On the other hand, if you set a goal to save $200 a week, that might be too lofty and unattainable for you. When you don't achieve that goal, you'll feel bad about yourself and may even give up on saving altogether. That's why it's important to set realistic financial goals that you can achieve.

Of course, we all have big dreams and aspirations. And that's great! But it's important to break those big dreams down into smaller, achievable chunks. Remember, "Rome wasn't built in a day". Set smaller goals that are achievable, give yourself small awards for achieving a goal, then gradually march toward your big dreams.

Stay In Control

To wrap up Chapter Three, the key to financial stability is to stay in control. Practical tips for staying in control include clearly understanding your financial obligations, setting a balanced budget, and saving up for a reserve fund. We have also looked at the concept of financial health check and I suggest keeping aside at least three months of living expenses as your reserve fund.

In Chapter Three we also looked at staying in control by avoiding impulse purchases, regularly reviewing your financial situation, be mindful about monthly subscriptions, cautious about credit card usage and settling debts on time. Remember that staying in control is an ongoing process and requires persistence and commitment.

Staying in control of your finances has numerous benefits, including reducing stress and anxiety, building financial security, and achieving long-term happiness. By setting realistic financial goals, creating a budget, and tracking your expenses, you can stay in control and avoid overspending and unmanageable debts.

By practicing and development of good financial habits, you can achieve your financial goals and live a happier, and financially secured life. So, set your own financial goals, create a budget, and take action to manage your financial well-being.

Development of good financial habits is essential for your long-term happiness. It takes time, effort, and persistence, but the benefits are well worth it. So, take charge and start managing your finances today, develop good habits and start working towards your financial goals.

Chapter Three (Day 3) Summary

In chapter three, we discussed the importance of building good financial habits and making smart decisions with our money. We talked about budgeting, saving, and avoiding debt. By developing healthy financial habits, we can reduce financial stress and achieve our long-term financial goals.

Now that we've covered how to take care of our finances, it's time to focus on taking care of our physical and mental health. In chapter four, we'll explore the importance of self-care, exercise, and maintaining a healthy work-life balance. By making small changes to our daily routines, we can improve our physical and mental well-being and live a happier, more fulfilling life. So, let's dive in and learn how to prioritize our health and well-being.

Chapter Four

HEALTH AND MENTAL WELL-BEING

"A sound mind in a sound body is a short but full description of a happy state in this world."

John Locke

Welcome to Chapter Four. In this chapter, we will explore the importance of maintaining both our physical and mental health. As women living alone, it's especially crucial that we prioritize our well-being in order to lead a self-contained life with pride. Not only do we want to feel good and be happy, but we also want our loved ones to be worry-free about our health. Let's be honest. Who doesn't want to be respected rather than pitied?

Taking care of our bodies and minds is not only important for our own well-being. It also allows us to live successful and fulfilling lives. When we feel good physically and mentally, we are more productive, energetic, and able to maintain positivity in tackling different challenges that come our way. It is important for us to stay strong, not only to support ourselves, but to be able to offer help to people around us.

I understand that life can get busy, and it is easy to put our health on the back burner. I know this far too well and luckily not too late. In this chapter, I'll provide you with some practical tips and advice to help you maintain your physical and mental health. From simple exercises to mindful practices, we will explore ways to help you feel good and lead a healthy life.

A Sad Story

Last week, I felt strange when I received a text message on my phone from an unknown number. The message read, "Hi Winnie. My name is Gabriella. I am the widow of your friend Gary, who recently passed away. Gary had mentioned your name from time to time in the past, praising your helpfulness and willingness to share advice when friends turn to you". Then Gabriella called and I took the opportunity to have a long chat with her. I couldn't offer much help other than my condolences. I was told that Gary had died of a sudden heart attack. I couldn't remember Gary's age and I didn't ask. I remember he was in his late thirties, which shocked me, as a friend of mine had died of a heart attack at that young age.

Gary was a successful young entrepreneur who ran a profitable business. His story has no direct relevance to this book. But his story reinforced my determination to write a good chapter about physical and mental health.

Sensible and Proper Diet

I must confess that I may not be the most qualified person to provide health advice. However, I urge you to give me your full attention, as I have learned from my mistakes. Just like machines require fuel, our bodies need nutrients. Regardless of whether you are a vegetarian, following a special diet plan, or refraining from certain foods due to allergies or religious reasons, it is essential to ensure that you consume a balanced and nutritious diet.

When you signed up for living alone, you have made a commitment to take care of yourself. We are adults, and it is generally believed that adults can look after ourselves. Unfortunately, that's not necessarily the case. Living alone means we have a lot on our plates. It can be easy to let our own health fall by the wayside as we focus on everything else that needs our attention. But the truth is, our physical and mental health should always be a top priority. After all, if we're not feeling our best, how can we possibly tackle other challenges in life?

Our bodies require a variety of nutrients to function properly. To keep us functioning and maintaining good physical health, we need to fuel our bodies with necessary nutrients. A healthy and balanced diet is essential or else we can experience a range of negative symptoms, from fatigue to headaches to digestive issues. Over time, this lack of proper nutrition can take a serious toll on our health.

I am sure the above information is nothing new to you. But why do so many of us still require regular reminders, and why does maintaining a healthy diet appear to be counterintuitive?

As mentioned earlier, our brains are wired to pursue happiness and pleasure. Our instinct is to seek comfort and immediate gratification, not necessarily with our best interests as the top consideration. Especially when life is busy, your brain may deceive you into pursuing food that is tasty, not necessarily wholesome, or something easy, not necessarily nutritious.

Brenda is an auditor, and she has a very busy schedule and always works long hours. By the time she arrives home at night, she is either too tired to cook or finds it too late to eat a proper meal. She sometimes fixes herself a sandwich with a glass of wine, or just some comfort food, such as microwave macaroni & cheese and ice-cream. Besides being overweight, Brenda encounters frequent headaches. In a recent body check, Brenda was found to have high blood pressure and high cholesterol problems. Brenda knows she needs to change her habit before her health develops other chronic conditions such as diabetes and heart disease.

I used to be underweighted. I don't eat much, and my appetite worsens when I'm tired. After a busy day, when I arrive home at eight or nine in the evening, the only thing I want is a drink and some snacks, such as dried fruits, cheese, and potato chips. Two years ago, I got a very bad flu, which took me two weeks to recover. The cough lingered for a long time, so my GP suggested I get a thorough check-up. The body check revealed that I was suffering from malnutrition. The report also showed early stages of osteoporosis. Can you believe someone living in the modern world, with its abundance of resources, could be suffering from malnutrition? Even I was shocked; it was a big wake-up call. I asked myself, "Regardless of how good I am as a co-worker, friend, daughter, etc., what value can I add if I don't even have a healthy body?"

Before continuing to read, I want you to take a moment to reflect. Are you looking after yourself? Do you prioritize your best interests? What is preventing you from being kind to yourself?

Never Skip a Proper Meal

I have a friend, Elsa, who is an amazing cook. She enjoys spending her weekends preparing food for herself and then uploading photos to social media. She spends hours preparing each meal, not counting the time she spends shopping for ingredients.

Are you like Elsa? Do you enjoy cooking? I believe many of you are more like me, who only enjoys preparing meals from time to time. You are likely to prefer eating simple meals so that you can save time for other activities you enjoy, such as reading a book, painting a picture, watching a movie, or doing some exercise. It is perfectly fine as long as you don't skip meals.

Skipping meals is something we all have done in the past while should be avoided. Skipping meals may seem like a simple and harmless way to cut calories or save time, but it can have serious negative effects on your health. In fact, skipping meals can be more harmful than you think.

Skipping meals will cause your blood sugar levels to drop. This leads to dizziness, headaches, and irritability. Both your tolerance level and your temper will worsen. That means your judgement and efficiency both decrease when your body doesn't have enough glucose (sugar) to fuel your brain and muscles. You will have difficulties concentrating. Therefore, it is important to remember that we must never make important decisions when we are hungry.

When your blood sugar level drops, the body will start drawing glucose from the liver. Once the liver reserve is drained, the body will start breaking down stored fats and converting them into glucose to provide energy. If this process continues for an extended period, the body will start breaking down muscle tissue. Over time, this will result in a loss of muscle mass and a slower metabolism. Worst of all, it increases the likelihood of developing diabetes and heart disease.

Another negative consequence of extended starvation is that the body enters "starvation mode." As a protective mechanism, your body reduces its metabolic rate to conserve energy. This means that when you next eat, your body is more likely to store the calories as fat, making it more difficult to lose weight over time.

Skipping proper meals and opting for comfort foods may disrupt the body's natural hunger and fullness cues, leading to overeating. When you skip a meal, you're more likely to feel excessively hungry at your next meal, leading you to overeat or make unhealthy food choices. This can quickly add up in terms of calories, leading to weight gain over time.

In the long term, unhealthy eating habits may lead to nutrient deficiencies. Our bodies require nutrients to function properly, including vitamins, minerals, and essential macronutrients like protein and carbohydrates. Being an independent and self-sufficient woman, the last thing we want is a weakened immune system, decreased muscle mass, and bone loss.

For women, nutrient deficiency may also have negative effects on our reproductive health, leading to irregular periods or missed periods, which can be a sign of hormonal imbalances in the body.

In conclusion, eat sensibly and do not skip a proper meal. It is not healthy nor sustainable. Develop the habit of maintaining a balanced and nutritious diet and practice moderation. Aim to eat regular, balanced meals throughout the day to keep your energy levels stable, maintain a healthy weight, and support your overall health and well-being. If you're short of time, you may try meal prepping or making quick, healthy meals like salads or stir-fries. By prioritizing regular meals, you'll set yourself up for better health and a more productive, fulfilling life. This is an ideal and sustainable lifestyle we all should pursue.

Work-life Balance

"All works and no play make Jack a dull boy". When I was small, I couldn't understand why someone would ever want "all work and no play". Now I am getting older, and I get to know better. It is because our brains are wired to pursue

happiness and satisfaction.

As we grow older, our sources of happiness and satisfaction become more complex. While children can feel happy from something as simple as a snack or a new toy, adults may pursue a sense of achievement, money rewards, recognition, and social status. Everyone has their own unique definition of happiness, but we have one thing in common, that things like good food, friendship, love, and entertainment can still bring us joy. However, we also crave a deeper sense of fulfillment. In this regard, it's important to understand why balancing work and play are essential for a happy and balanced life.

Now, it's story time again. It goes back to my university days, when I started to realize I was a perfectionist. I was young and didn't realize that the concept of "perfection" simply doesn't exist in the real world. I set myself challenges and tried to get "the best" transcript that could make me feel proud. I forced myself to work nonstop, writing, reviewing, and modifying a piece of work until the deadline for submission. To maximize my time, I refrained from any form of entertainment, considering that it was a waste of my time. It wasn't until my final year that I realized my temper was bad and I easily got irritated. My best friend noticed the problem and suggested I go see a therapist. I took her advice, and after a few sessions, the therapist told me that I had been driving myself too hard. She asked me to give myself a break, but at first I refused, telling her I couldn't or else my results would decline. She encouraged me to start by giving myself a few hours of rest every week.

I cautiously took up the therapist's advice. I started by giving myself a two-week trial period and observing whether my performance degraded before gradually increasing the break time until I found an equilibrium. To my amazement, this action completely changed my perspective on work-life balance. By allowing myself to take a day off at the weekend and simply enjoy life, my performance peaked, and my emotional and mental health quickly recovered.

As mentioned before, human brains are wired to pursue happiness. If you want to give the best of yourself, you need to feel good, that includes both physical and mental health.

Entertainment is a vital part for maintaining a healthy and happy life. If you want top performance, give yourself enough mental "nutrients". You need to feel good to reach your peak performance. I encourage you to learn how to strike the balance that works best for you.

Rest and Sleep

Getting enough sleep is not just about feeling rested and energized. Sleeping plays a crucial role in maintaining physical and mental health. Research shows that lack of sleep can lead to a range of health issues. Your immune system may be weakened and there will be an increased risk of chronic diseases like diabetes and heart disease. Your mental health is also at risk such as anxiety and depression.

It is commonly believed that adults require an average of eight hours of sleep every day. I conducted some in-depth research online and found out that the actual amount of sleep required can vary from person to person. There is no universally agreed-upon magical number. It was said that adults between the ages of 18 and 64 should aim for 7 to 9 hours of sleep per night. In other words, eight hours is only an average number. In fact, some people can feel rested after as few as six hours of sleep, while others may need as much as ten. Age, genetics, lifestyle, and overall health are factors that cause the deviations.

Whether you are a night owl or an early riser, you should establish your own routine that allows you to get enough sleep. Stay up late at night is not an option if you have a job that requires you to work during the day, On the other hand, if you are a freelancer or have a more flexible work schedule, you have the opportunity to tailor your sleeping routine to suit your individual preference. However, it is important to resist the temptation to sacrifice sleep for work or other activities. Remember that quality work and productivity are more achievable when you are well-rested and have a clear mind.

It is our own responsibility to ensure we get enough sleep every day disregard our work or lifestyles. Rest and sleep are essential for maintaining a healthy mind and body. Sleeping helps recharge our bodies and allows us to be more productive at work. Quality of work is more important than the time spent at work. So, make sure you take enough rest to maintain the quality of your work. Your mind and body will thank you for it, and you will be better equipped to face everyday challenges. A clear and focused mind is especially crucial when you are required to make important or difficult decisions.

Insufficient rest can lead to poor concentration, which in turn can lead to mistakes. Stay away from important decisions when you're tired and drained, or else you are more likely to make a decision that you will regret later. Even for noncritical decisions, it is no good in making silly mistakes that could have easily been avoided. That's why it's important to prioritize your rest and sleep and give yourself enough time to recover.

But that doesn't mean you should spend all your free time sleeping. Balance work and play and give yourself enough "pleasure" to keep your brain happy. Don't forget to prioritize your rest and sleep and make time for things you enjoy. After all, all work and no play make Jack a dull boy, and we don't want to become a dull girl, do we? So, go out there and have some fun! Whether it's reading a good book, watching your favorite TV show, or spending time with loved ones, make sure you always make time to do things you enjoy. If you don't, your brain will protest and make it harder for you to concentrate at work later.

Remember, mental health is just as important as physical health. Taking the time to relax and enjoy yourself can enhance your health and happiness in general. Always keep in mind the importance of getting sufficient rest and never forget to make time for activities that bring you joy. Your body, soul, and mind will experience satisfaction, and you will live a joyful, sustainable lifestyle that you will appreciate and that others will admire.

Develop an Exercise Routine

If there is one investment that would certainly give you a positive return in life, it is exercise. Yes, I see exercise as an investment as you need to put in your time, your effort, and your commitment, then you wait to see the positive outcomes. For someone like me, who isn't a natural-born athlete, this process does not happen naturally, and it takes a lot of self-discipline and hard work, but if you incorporate regular exercise into your life, that can make a significant impact on your life quality.

I have been thinking how I could possibly write this section and attract you to carry on reading. Everyone knows exercise is incredibly important for our health, yet not many people maintain an exercise regime. We all realize that exercise helps us maintain a healthy weight, that exercise helps lower our risk for many chronic diseases, such as heart disease, type II diabetes, and certain types of cancer. Plus, regular exercise can improve our mental health, helping to alleviate stress, anxiety, and depression. But why it is easier said than done?

We all know that exercise is good for us, yet many of us still find ways to procrastinate and avoid it like it's a root canal. Perhaps it's because the idea of working up a sweat and feeling the burn just doesn't appeal to us at the moment. Or maybe it's the fear of being judged by the gym rats and fitness gurus. Whatever the reason, we often find ourselves escaping from exercise, convincing ourselves that we'll start tomorrow or next week. But tomorrow turns into next month, and before we know it, we're back on the couch, binge-watching TV shows and chowing down on potato chips. It is because your brain has not yet tasted the pleasure and joy brought about by exercise and therefore it tempts you into pursuing other pleasures that give you satisfaction that your brain is familiar with. It's a vicious cycle that we've all been guilty of at some point or another. But the truth is, the longer we put off exercise, the harder it becomes to get started. It's time to break the cycle and start making exercise a priority in our lives.

Here below please find some tricks that have worked for me. Let me share with you and hope that you can break away from the procrastination cycle and get started on your exercise journey. Firstly, start small. You don't need to sign up for a marathon or start lifting heavy weights from the get-go. Begin with a 10-minute walk or a gentle yoga class. Secondly, find a workout buddy or a community to join. Having someone to hold you accountable and motivate you can make all the difference. Thirdly, make exercise a non-negotiable part of your routine. Treat it like an important appointment that cannot be missed. Finally, don't beat yourself up if you miss a day or two. Just get back on track as soon as possible and keep moving forward. Remember, the hardest part is getting started, but once you do, the benefits will speak for themselves. Then comes the last step, which is crucially important. After 4 weeks of regular exercise, go to your full-length mirror naked. See the results and admire the small and subtle changes that you have made. So, now take that first step, and before you know it, exercise will become a regular and enjoyable part of your life.

Are you eager to start? I am happy that you are still reading. To make sure you can stick with your exercise routine, it is important to pick an exercise that suits you. In case you prefer to exercise outdoors, you may want to select activities such as hiking or running. Or if you prefer the comfort of an indoor environment, then a gym with equipment such as weights or cardio machines could be your choice. It's all about finding what works for you. Understanding your own body condition is also important in choosing the right type of exercise. If you have joint problems, avoid jogging as it gives pressure to your ankles and knees. In fact, if you are not a fan of high-intensity exercises, stretching, yoga, and Pilates can still be extremely beneficial.

Remember developing an exercise regime is to set aside time for it and stick to it. By doing this, you make exercise a habit rather than a chore. You may want to give yourself some extra motivation. Try developing an incentive program for yourself, such as rewarding yourself with a new workout outfit or a massage after reaching a certain milestone. But please avoid rewarding yourself with a big meal or some desserts or else it will defeat the purpose. I know you won't!

Remember, exercise doesn't have to be a dreaded task. It can be a fun and enjoyable part of your daily routine. So, whether you're a seasoned athlete or a beginner just starting out, there's no better time to start developing an exercise regime that fits you and your lifestyle. Trust me, both your body and mind will benefit from it!

Associate with Positive Friends

As social creatures, it's natural for us to seek connection and support from those around us. And there's no denying that having positive friends can make all the difference in our lives. After all, who doesn't love being around people who uplift and inspire us, who make us feel good about ourselves, and who help us see the brighter side of life?

But what about those negative friends—the ones who always seem to bring us down? We all have them, whether it's the co-worker who complains endlessly about their job, or the relative who's constantly stirring up drama. And while it may be tempting to keep them around out of a sense of obligation or loyalty, the truth is that negative energy can be just as contagious as bacteria. In fact, studies have shown that negative emotions and moods can spread from person to person like a virus.

At my twenties, I met a girl named Rachel. At first, I thought she was a nice person to be around. However, as time went by, I began to realize that she was always complaining about something. She would complain about her job, her friends, her family, and even the weather.

One day, Rachel was telling me about her boss. She was saying how her boss was so unappreciative of her hard work and how he always gave her extra work to do. I listened and tried to be supportive, but I noticed that this was a pattern. Every time we met, Rachel had a new complaint about someone or something.

I started to feel exhausted being around her. Her negative energy was like a dark cloud that followed her everywhere. I realized that her complaints were affecting my own mood and attitude. I started to distance myself from her. At first, I felt guilty about pulling away. But then I realized that I couldn't let her negative energy bring me down. I needed to surround myself with positive people and positive energy.

I made a conscious effort to spend time with people who had a positive outlook on life. I started to notice how much better I felt when I was around them. As for Rachel, I still see her from time to time nowadays. I am mature and more sophisticated now. I am no longer easily brought down by her negativity. But I still make sure to limit my interactions with Rachel. I would try to redirect the conversation to more positive topics, but if she continued to complain, I would politely end the conversation.

Over these years, I realized that it's important to surround ourselves with positive energy. Negative people can drain us of our own energy and bring us down. It's okay to be supportive and try to help others, but we also need to take care of ourselves and our own mental health.

How then can we escape the cycle of negativity and instead surround ourselves with positive energy? First and foremost, it is essential to remember that we are emotional beings and that it is acceptable to share our emotions with our friends.

However, we must also be careful not to make this a habit. When we repeatedly tell our minds that we are sad and seek consolation from others, we reinforce these negative emotions and increase their likelihood of persisting.

Instead, surround yourself with individuals who motivate you to be your best self and who exude positivity. This could include acquaintances, relatives, or even co-workers who share your values and interests. Whether a yoga class, a book club, or a community service initiative, seek out social activities that uplift you. And don't be afraid to establish boundaries with friends or acquaintances who deplete your energy or bring you down.

Obviously, it is also essential to remember that nobody is flawless and that we all experience bad days. By choosing to associate with positive people and cultivating a positive mindset, however, we can generate a ripple effect of positive energy that extends throughout our social networks. Who knows? Perhaps if we surround ourselves with positive companions, we will inspire others to do the same!

Mental Health and Well-being

When was the last time you felt regretful about living on your own? For me, the last time that happened was when I was sick. Remember I told you that I had a really bad flu two years ago? I coughed badly and had a high fever. My muscles ached, and even going to the kitchen to get a glass of water was torture. At that time, I so much hoped that there was someone else in the house. Have you experienced something similar before? This is because when you are physically ill, your mental state becomes fragile.

As a culture, we often focus so much on our physical health that we forget how important it is to take care of our mental health. But why is it so essential to maintain mental health? To begin with, let's state the obvious: when we are physically ill, our mental condition can become extremely fragile. When we're ill or in agony, it's difficult to maintain a positive attitude. Even if we are physically robust, however, there are other aspects of life that can drain us. Workplace stress, relationship issues, and financial difficulties are just a few of the factors that can negatively impact our mental health.

As previously discussed, rule number one for mental well-being is to surround ourselves with positive individuals. You know who they are—those acquaintances and relatives who always seem to make us feel better. Time spent with these individuals can uplift our mental health. On the other hand, we should avoid negative individuals who bring us down. Negative thoughts and emotions can be contagious, much like a contagious disease.

Apart from surrounding ourselves with positivity, you may try to cultivate mindfulness. Mindfulness is a mental state achieved by focusing one's awareness on the present moment. It involves being aware of and attentive to one's surroundings, thoughts, and emotions, without judgment or distraction. Mindfulness has been adapted into mainstream psychology and self-help techniques to reduce stress, anxiety, and improve mental and physical health. This can take many forms, including yoga, meditation, and profound breathing exercises. The key is to discover something that works and incorporate it into your daily routine. Mindfulness can help us remain grounded, reduce tension and anxiety, and enhance our mental health.

But what happens if your mental situation worsens? If you suspect you are experiencing symptoms of depression or anxiety, you should immediately seek professional assistance. Don't wait until things spiral out of control; the sooner you seek assistance, the quicker you will recover. Psychotherapy can be extremely beneficial for one's mental health. You must not feel ashamed to seek assistance when you need it.

Let's remember that, just like physical health, mental health requires our attention and care. The number one rule is to surround yourself with positive people. Practicing mindfulness is also an effective and proven strategy. Last but not least, don't hesitate to seek professional help if necessary. With these tools, your life will be happier and healthier in the long run.

Avoid Social Media When Feeling Despair

Social media has become an integral part of our lives, but let's face it: it's not always sunshine and rainbows. As humans, we all have our ups and downs, but social media has a way of magnifying these emotions. When we're feeling down, it's easy to start comparing our lives to the carefully curated and filtered versions of others' lives that we see online. This is why, when you're feeling despair, it's best to take a step back from social media.

Let's be honest: people tend to post only happy things on social media. It's like an arena for people to show off their successes, but rarely do we see people posting about their failures or struggles. So, when you're feeling down, scrolling through your newsfeed can be a real bummer. You don't want to see someone's expensive birthday gift when you're struggling with financial problems. You don't want to see honeymooners when you just broke up with your partner. It's enough to make you feel even more miserable.

And speaking of feeling miserable, you must resist the temptation to vent your frustrations on social media. Sure, you might get some sympathy likes and comments, but that's not real consolation. Social media is not built for interactive consolation, and you're unlikely to find any real solutions to your problems there.

You should stay away from social media when you are upset. Take this time to do something that makes you feel good. You may go for a walk, listen to some music, read a book, or take a hot bath. These types of activities could comfort you and distract you from your problems. When I feel miserable, I like to watch comedy shows. Alternatively, you can reach out to a trusted family member or friend. Sometimes, just talking to people you trust can help you feel better.

In sum, it is best to avoid social media when you are depressed. The meticulously curated versions of other people's lives we see online can be overwhelming and make us feel inferior. Instead, temporarily disconnect from the noise of the outside world for a while and give yourself a pamper. Practice mindfulness and surround yourself with positive energy. And remember, if you are truly struggling, do not hesitate to talk to people you trust or seek professional assistance. Your mental health is equally important as your physical health, so take care of yourself!

Chapter Four (Day 4) Summary

In Chapter Four, we explored the importance of maintaining good physical and mental health. We discussed the benefits of regular exercise, mindfulness, positive social relationships, and good sleeping habits. We also highlighted the importance of a balanced diet. By following these guidelines, you can improve your overall well-being and live a more fulfilling life.

Now that we've discussed the importance of physical and mental health, let's move on to Chapter Five where we'll focus on the importance of maintaining strong relationships and a support network. We'll explore the benefits of having a close network of friends and/or family, as well as the strategies for building and nurturing those relationships.

We'll also discuss the challenges of maintaining healthy relationships in the digital age and offer tips for overcoming those obstacles. So, let's dive in and learn how to build stronger, more meaningful connections in our lives.

Chapter Five

FRIENDS AND RELATIONS

"Walking with a friend in the dark is better than walking alone in the light."

Helen Keller

Everyone, regardless of whether they are introverts or extroverts, desires affection and connection. On our voyage through life, we meet numerous individuals, with some of whom we develop attachments. These are known as friendships. A genuine friend is someone who is there for you in both good and bad times, providing happiness, support, and company. It is essential that we surround ourselves with reliable and trustworthy individuals and that we offer them our own affection and support in return. Cultivating and maintaining intimate relationships is essential for all individuals, not just women who live alone.

In this chapter, we will explore the power of friendship and why it is crucial to our well-being. We'll look at how strong relationships can help us through difficult times and how they contribute to our happiness and success. We will also examine the qualities that make a good friend and how to cultivate these qualities in ourselves.

In addition to discussing friendship, we will also delve into the topic of relationships. While friendships provide us with companionship and support, romantic relationships have the potential to provide us with a deeper level of intimacy and connection. However, they also require more work and commitment. We will discuss the importance of healthy communication, mutual respect, and trust in romantic relationships.

This chapter provides an overview and insights for the development of strong and long-lasting relationships with the people in your life. If you wish to strengthen existing friendships, establish a support network of friends and family, or develop meaningful romantic relationships, I dedicate this chapter to you.

Who is Your True Friend?

Can you name five friends who you regard to be your closest buddies? Do you find it easy or difficult? Is it challenging for you to come up with five? Or do you have more than five best friends and find it difficult to rank in the top five?

We all have friends. Your closest friend may not be the person you've known the longest, but he or she is likely someone who has accompanied you through some of your life's most memorable experiences. It takes time to cultivate a friendship, but only a minor misunderstanding can destroy it. Therefore, please hold your friendship in high regard. It is not a mere coincidence.

A good friend is someone you can rely on, regardless of what life throws at you. They are the individuals with whom you can confidently share your joy and sadness, knowing they will always be there for you. A true friend is someone you can rely on and trust, who you will think of when you are happy or sad, and who will give you honest feedback, even when some feedback may not be pleasant.

When you come across something unusual in life, whether it is a new opportunity or a challenge, you want to share it with your best friend. You know that he or she is understanding and willing to listen. No matter how trivial your thoughts may be, you want to hear his or her opinion. And when you need them, they do their best to make time for you. Whether it be a quick phone call or a long chat over coffee, a true friend is there to support you through thick and thin.

The beauty of a genuine friendship is that there is no price tag or condition attached to it. You are there for each other simply because you care about one another. You consider your friend's benefit sometimes even before your own, and vice versa. It's a bond that goes beyond any material possessions or status symbols.

Another sign of a true friend is your willingness to share your failures and embarrassments with them. You know you don't need to worry about being judged. A good friend is someone who lifts you up when you fall, who does not make you feel ashamed for your mistakes. You can be vulnerable with a good friend and willing to turn to him or her for help whenever you feel you need it.

Now you have answers about who your best friends are. They are people who stood by your side during difficult times. They have witnessed your strengths and weaknesses and have been there when you need them. It is essential to cherish and maintain these relationships. Take the time to acknowledge them for their support and to express how much they mean to you.

Our Commitment to a Friend

As human beings, we all desire companionship. We enjoy the sense of security that comes with having good friends. Once you have found a true friend, it is essential to cherish the relationship. But what exactly does it mean to be committed to a friendship? Here are some of the most important promises we must make to our companions.

Firstly, we must understand that friendship is reciprocal but not an exchange. We shouldn't treat our friends well just because we want them to be good to us in return. Being a good friend means being consistently supportive, trustworthy, and reliable.

One of the most important commitments we can make to our friends is to be someone they can confide in. We must promise to keep our friends' secrets safe and not disclose their matters to a third party. This is the foundation of trust in any friendship.

Another very important duty is to always treat our friends with respect and love. We must not judge a friend, no matter what he or she says. We should strive to be a positive influence in their lives and do our best to provide an environment where they can be themselves without fear of rejection or criticism.

Being a loyal friend also involves being available when needed. Even if it means answering a call at an inconvenient time, we must lend our ears. We must offer our counsel but recognize that our friends may not always follow it. Sometimes, the best way to support a friend is to simply listen.

Additionally, we must be willing to give our honest opinion when something is incorrect. This does not necessitate hurting our friend's emotions, but rather providing an alternative viewpoint to assist them in avoiding errors. Even if it's not what they want to hear, a genuine friend will appreciate our candor.

It's important to make time for each other in order to maintain strong friendships. This means setting aside time to catch up from time to time. We should celebrate our friends' successes and support them through their struggles.

Finally, we must be willing to forgive our friends when they make mistakes and to apologize when we make mistakes ourselves. No friendship is perfect, but if we are committed to being good friends, we can work through any issues that arise.

I hope my closest friend is reading this chapter. I wish to express my gratitude for her friendship throughout these years. I am here to honor her friendship and I promise to be the best friend I can be. Thank you for your incredibly valuable support. Thank you, Amigo!

The Inner Circle

We all know that not all friendships are equal. We have friends who are merely acquaintances, while others have earned a position among us as close friends. We tend to consider these friends our "inner circle". Understanding that different friends have different limits, or in other words, different boundaries, enables us to set reasonable expectations for our relationships so as to avoid disappointment. We must not have the wrong expectation that everyone will fit into our inner circle, and that's okay. We can continue to value and enjoy our casual friendships while also giving certain priorities to those who have a strong bond with us.

Regarding friendships, it is essential to observe boundaries and avoid asking for favors that go beyond the extent of the relationship. We must never place our friends in difficult situations by making unreasonable requests. We must communicate openly and truthfully with our friends regarding our needs and boundaries, and we must also respect theirs. Otherwise, we risk straining our friendship. Even if we provide others with consistent assistance, we must remember that the situation is not always reciprocal.

If you have a genuine companion who is consistently generous and supportive, you are extraordinarily fortunate, and this is likely one of the greatest gifts you will receive. You should be thankful for having a friend who is always there for you, from small acts of compassion to crucial situations. It is crucial to recognize and appreciate these acts of generosity from our friends and not take them for granted. Expressing gratitude and showing appreciation can strengthen our friendships and deepen our connection.

Having a true buddy who is regularly helpful, and kind is a tremendous blessing. Among the best presents you'll ever get; this must be near the top of the list. Whether it's a small favor or a major life event, you should be thankful for the friend who is always there for you. Please don't take your friend for granted. Recognizing and appreciating these gestures through words and deeds of gratitude is crucial. Showing genuine gratitude can improve bonds and foster more cooperation.

Even the closest of friends may not always be able to fulfill our requests or meet our expectations. It's important to understand that our friends have their own lives, priorities, and limitations, and we shouldn't take it personally if they can't always be there for us in the way we might like. Instead, we should respect their decisions and choices and maintain a positive attitude towards our friendships even when things don't go according to plan.

Just as it's important to respect our friends' boundaries, it's equally important to set and maintain our own. It is okay to turn down a request if we're not comfortable with one that a friend makes. Learning to say no politely and respectfully can help us avoid resentment, burnout, and other negative consequences. It's important to communicate clearly and honestly with our friends about our boundaries and to be open to negotiation when appropriate.

Our inner circle of friends is a vital and valuable part of our lives. It's important to be intentional and careful about who we invite into this space. These are the ones who have proven to be loyal and supportive. They are the people we most trust. The people who are closest to us in our social circle hold a special place in our hearts. We need to be selective and deliberate about who we let into this room. You can count on these people to always have your back. These are the people in our lives with whom we can always confide and be completely honest. However, even amongst our closest friends and family members, it is essential that we all learn to set and adhere to healthy boundaries. Investing time and energy into cultivating meaningful connections pays off in spades.

In summary, our inner circle of friends is a valuable and

precious part of our lives. We can strengthen and deepen these relationships by respecting boundaries, showing gratitude, and communicating honestly. At the same time, it's important to be mindful of our own needs and boundaries and to be intentional about who we invite into our inner circle. By doing so, we can cultivate a safe and strong support network.

Our Support Network

In the previous section, the concept of a "support network" was introduced. What does "support network" mean to you? In my opinion, it's something like a trapeze artist's safety net.

Your support network, which is made up of a group of trustworthy people, is crucial for your convenience and well-being. People in your support network might be members of your family, friends, co-workers, old acquaintances, or, quite often, your neighbors. Individuals in your support network do not need to be from your inner circle; in fact, they likely are not. People who are part of your support system may or may not be close friends or family members, while your network of friends should be composed of people you can trust and who are also eager to lend a hand when you need it.

My immediate neighbors are a young married couple, and they are a crucial part of my support network. When one of us is traveling overseas, we take care of the other's mail by clearing out mailboxes. My friend who works as a therapist checks in with me occasionally, for a talk over the phone. Annie, my former coworker who now lives in the same neighborhood, is kind enough to run errands for me on occasion when she knows that I need to stay up late in order to meet project deadlines.

Building a strong support network is like being in a relay race where everyone needs to pass the baton. You can't be the only one running, or you'll end up running out of steam. It's important to find people who can pick up the baton when you're feeling tired or overwhelmed. And when your friends need a break, you can return the favor and carry the baton for them.

Think of it like building a pyramid. Each person supports the one above them, and together they form a strong, stable structure. Just like in a pyramid, every person in your support network has a unique role to play. Maybe your best friend is your rock, always there to offer a shoulder to cry on. Maybe your sister is the one who keeps you grounded, reminding you of what's truly important. And maybe your coworker is the one who always makes you laugh, helping you keep things in perspective.

But building a support network isn't just about finding people who can support you. It's also about being there for others. It's about offering a listening ear when a friend needs to vent or a helping hand when they're struggling. It's about being the one who can make them laugh or who can offer a fresh perspective on a difficult problem. When we're there for others, they're more likely to be there for us when we need them.

Remember, building a support network takes time and effort. It's not something that happens overnight, but it's worth investing in. As the saying goes, "If you want to go fast, go alone. If you want to go far, go together." And when you have a strong support network, you can go farther than you ever thought possible.

Cherish and Nurture Friendship

The bond of friendship is precious. It's like tending to a plant so that it might grow and flourish. Our friendships are like gardens; they thrive when given time, care, and love. Get your gardening tools ready because it's time to start caring for your friendships.

We should value our friendships. Through friendship we obtain tremendous support, free advice, and honest feedback. They cheer for us when we win and console us when we lose. They always have our backs, they make us laugh, and they listen to our rants. True friendship is priceless, and we should treat our friends as such.

Friends are precious, but we must not take them for granted. Friendships, like plants, thrive when they receive regular attention. We must make an effort to keep in touch, not lose track of crucial dates, and often check in with our pals. Small acts of kindness are equally as meaningful as grand ones. It's easy to show our friends how much we appreciate them with just a few words, a card, or a spontaneous visit.

Of course, the purpose of a friendship goes beyond material gain. Our ability to contribute is also crucial. When our friends really need us, not just when it's convenient for us, we need to be there for them. It's not always simple, but it's always worthwhile to try your best. We need to work on our listening skills, give others our whole attention when they need us, and offer assistance whenever we can.

Nonetheless, confines must be respected. We should be considerate of our friends' feelings and wants, and we should always seek their consent before offering advice. Please remember that friends choose to confide in us or listen to our advice because they trust us. Do not abuse their trust. Sometimes when our friends don't want to talk, just be there to show support. Our company and empathy could mean a lot to a friend.

Loving our friends "their way" is crucial to nurturing and maintaining our friendships. Just like any other relationship, we need to respect and appreciate our friends' preferences and boundaries. It means understanding what they enjoy and dislike and making an effort to accommodate their wishes. For instance, if your friend is a bookworm, you can surprise her with a new book she's been wanting to read. If your friend values privacy, give her space and don't pry into her personal life. It's about being attuned to their needs and wants and showing them that we care about them in a way that's meaningful to them.

Defend Your Friendship

When it comes to building long term interpersonal relationship, defending your friendship is essential. This means being willing to stand up for your friends when they need it and being an advocate for them in your shared circles. It also means avoiding second-guessing and always seeking clarification before getting angry or upset with your friends. Misunderstandings happen, but the key is to communicate openly and honestly to avoid any unnecessary tension.

It is possible for good friends to get too close to each other's boundaries. When this happens, remember to express our feelings when things make us uneasy or go beyond our limits. This way, we can avoid feeling resentful or overextended in our relationships.

We live in a society, interacting with different people every day. It is possible for us to hear negative things about our friends. We must feel with our own hearts and judge with our own eyes, and we must resist believing rumors.

Sometimes, people can be quick to judge and spread gossip, but as true friends, we should value each other's privacy and respect each other's boundaries.

Additionally, being open to sharing feedback is an important part of building and maintaining healthy friendships. When it comes to negative feedback, it's essential to tailor our words carefully and communicate with kindness and empathy. Remember, our friends are human too, and we all have areas where we can improve.

In conclusion, building a strong support network requires effort and commitment from both sides. We must defend our friendships, communicate openly and honestly, be generous and willing to share, and respect each other's boundaries. By doing so, we can create a circle of friends that lifts us up, supports us through life's challenges, and brings us immeasurable joy and fulfillment.

Be a Good Listener

Being loved and cared for is something that every human being craves, but this need can be overwhelming from time to time. Having a strong social support system is essential to our health and happiness. Friends are the people we turn to for assistance in times of need, and we do the same for them.

Simply being present and listening can sometimes be the most helpful thing we can do. As I've gotten older, I've realized that my friends don't always want advice; they simply want someone to talk to. They only require someone they can trust to listen to them as they think out loud.

Therein lies the need to listen attentively. It's important to get into the habit of paying attention and responding thoughtfully when your friends are talking to you. Being an excellent listener makes you a treasured companion. Friendships are priceless, and the respect and trust you earn from them will be priceless as well.

Remember that part of being a good friend is not disclosing the details of your conversation with them to others. Maintaining trust and developing a solid connection depends on keeping private information just that: private.

Therefore, let us all strive to be the kind of friends that we would like to have, offering support and listening when our friends need it most. Always keep in mind that you can't celebrate your success, happiness, and fulfillment on your own.

Allow Friends to Help

When I was younger, I used to believe that being independent and strong was the best way to gain respect and admiration. However, as I grew older, I realized how vital it is to be approachable and exhibit our human side in order to develop genuine connections with others. We are social beings and most of us want meaningful human interactions.

Offering assistance to individuals in need is one way to establish and strengthen interpersonal bonds. Being there for our friends, whether it's offering a listening ear or assisting with a chore, is a vital component of friendship.

But it's also crucial to acknowledge that we, too, require assistance from time to time. We should never be ashamed or embarrassed to seek assistance when we need it. Our friends are there to support us in good and bad times and enabling them to assist us strengthen our bonds.

However, keep in mind that friendship is a two-way street. We should never take advantage of our friends' generosity and goodwill. Instead, we should seek to establish a mutually beneficial connection in which we both contribute and receive support, love, and affection.

Finally, developing and keeping lasting friendships necessitates being authentic, vulnerable, and open to giving and receiving assistance. This way, we can make deep and profound friendships that will last a lifetime.

Start of a Relationship

Let's talk about romance. It's natural to feel attracted to someone and want to pursue a relationship, but it's important to protect yourself as well. Here are some tips that I've learned along the way that might be helpful for you too.

Firstly, take it slow. Don't bring someone home the first time you meet, even if you have common friends. Get to know them better and make sure you feel comfortable around them before inviting them into your personal space.

Another important point is to keep valuables out of sight when someone new comes over. While most people are trustworthy, it's better to err on the side of caution.

It's also important not to reveal too much too soon. There's plenty to talk about in the early stages of a relationship, such as hobbies, common interests, and childhood memories. However, be cautious about disclosing sensitive personal information, such as your income or other private details.

Lastly, it's important to be mindful about who you give your keys to. It's easy to hand them over in a moment of trust or excitement, but it can be difficult to get them back if things go sour. My friend Linda once gave her keys to a guy she'd only known for two weeks, and it turned out he was seeing multiple people at once. Even when he returned the keys, Linda didn't feel safe and ended up having to change all her locks.

So, be cautious and take your time when it comes to developing a romantic relationship. Remember, you are in control of your own safety and well-being.

Protect Yourself

To protect yourself in friendships and relationships, you have to find a balance between being sincere and not letting yourself be used. Every relationship needs trust, but it's important to be careful, especially when it comes to money. Now, I'm not saying you should be like Ebenezer Scrooge or anything. We all want to help our friends when they are in trouble. But you need to think about a few things before you pull out your wallet.

First, you should figure out how much you can afford to give. Make sure the amount you're offering is something you can give up without putting a strain on your finances or your own well-being. Second, think about the kind of friendship you have. Have you been friends with this person for a long time and built up a lot of trust? Or is this connection not that old? While there's no fixed time frame for determining trust, it's important to be cautious when dealing with friendships that haven't stood the test of time.

I've come to think that any money I lend is a gift, so I treat it that way. So, if the person can't pay me back, I won't be stressed out or angry. But hey, that's just how I do things. Everyone has a different amount of comfort when it comes to lending money.

I have had bad experiences before, that friends didn't repay the debts and those were significant amounts. But let me tell you about my friend Maple. She had experienced something so bad that was much worse than mine. Maple gave all of her money to a coworker who said she needed it for chemotherapy for her mother. It turned out to be a lie, which was very sad. Later, it was found out that this coworker had taken advantage of the kindness of many others by borrowing money from them under false pretenses. Maple was hurt both personally and financially by what happened. She ended up losing everything she had saved, which made her sad and she had to seek therapy to overcome the depression it caused.

When it comes to money, these stories serve as reminders of how important it is for friends to set clear standards and limits. By doing this, you can protect your friendships and keep yourself from going through unnecessary pain. Remember that it's not about being mean or self-centered; it's about protecting your own well-being and keeping good relationships based on trust and respect.

Your Digital Presence

Our internet presence is equally as crucial as our physical one in today's digital world. We must be mindful of the dangers of providing personal information online. When dealing with our online presence, we must maintain a feeling of data privacy. This entails being cautious about what we communicate on social media and refraining from sharing too much personal information. Remember, once something is out there, it's there for good.

Another thing that we should be aware of is that text-based communication can often lead to misunderstandings, so double-check with the person you're conversing with when in doubt. Don't make any assumptions. Minor misunderstandings, such as receiving the wrong place or time, might cause discomfort. A major misunderstanding could lead to the end of a relationship. It happened to me a couple of times that my mom misinterpreted my text messages and got angry with me. I wasn't aware until I called her up one week later, but she has been upset for one whole week which was completely avoidable.

Another important reminder is to always seek confirmation when something appears suspicious. Let me share the story of my friend Cathy, who unfortunately fell victim to a cunning hacker. This hacker managed to infiltrate her friend's Facebook account and deceived Cathy into revealing her credit card information. It was only when Cathy received a call from her credit card company about an unusual transaction that she realized what had happened. This incident serves as a powerful reminder that we need to be cautious when sharing sensitive information, especially in plain text. Taking that extra step to confirm the legitimacy of requests can help protect you from falling prey to online scams and safeguard your personal information.

Well, online presence isn't always bad, sometimes it can be rather beneficial, especially if you're working from home and don't have the opportunity to interact with people face-to-face on a daily basis. In such cases, it can be helpful to establish a regular line of communication with someone you trust. For example, you could set up a daily routine of exchanging "good morning" greetings. This simple gesture serves as a way for your friend to check in on you and ensure that everything is alright if they notice you haven't been online as frequently. It's like having a virtual support system, ready to lend a hand when needed.

Remember that your online presence is equally as vital as your physical presence. Maintain vigilance and safeguard your privacy and personal information.

Chapter Five (Day 5) Summary

In Chapter Five, we explored the importance of building strong friendships and relationships in our lives. We discussed the significance of having a support network and the value it brings to our overall well-being. We emphasized the importance of reciprocity, trust, and open communication in maintaining healthy connections with others. Additionally, we delved into the significance of cherishing and nurturing our friendships, as well as the need to set boundaries and respect each other's privacy. We also touched upon the importance of being vigilant when it comes to our digital presence and safeguarding our personal information. Overall, this chapter serves as a guide to cultivating meaningful relationships and creating a support system that contributes to our happiness and fulfillment.

Key Takeaway Points:

- Building strong friendships and relationships is crucial for our overall well-being.
- Reciprocity, trust, and open communication are the foundations of healthy connections.
- Cherish and nurture your friendships, being mindful of each other's needs and boundaries.
- Safeguard your personal information and be cautious with your digital presence.
- Cultivate a support network that provides love, support, and understanding in times of need.

Remember, relationships are a vital part of our lives, and investing in them can bring immense joy and fulfillment.

Chapter Six

THE GREATEST LOVE OF ALL

"Self-care is not selfish or self-indulgent. We cannot nurture others from a dry well. We need to take care of our own needs first, then we can give from our surplus, our abundance."

Jennifer Louden

In previous chapters, we laid the groundwork for building a secure and satisfying existence. We began by examining our physical safety, then our financial well-being, and then our relationships with others. Now is the time to progress further on our journey. Chapter Six explores the transformative power of self-love.

I'm confident the concept of self-love is not new to you. What is the meaning of self-love to you? Self-love transcends fundamental self-care. It is about cultivating a profound sense of self-compassion, acceptance, and benevolence. It involves recognizing our value, celebrating our strengths, and accepting our flaws. True emotional security and interior tranquillity cannot be attained without self-love.

Throughout this chapter, we will explore various facets of self-love and discover practical strategies to cultivate it in our daily lives. We will delve into the importance of self-acceptance and self-compassion, recognizing that we are deserving of love and kindness just as much as anyone else. By nurturing a healthy relationship with ourselves, we can enhance our overall well-being and create a positive ripple effect in all aspects of our lives.

Self-love also involves setting healthy boundaries and prioritizing our own needs. We will explore the concept of self-care and the importance of carving out dedicated time for activities that bring us joy and rejuvenation. From engaging in hobbies that ignite our passions to practicing mindfulness and self-reflection, we will unlock the keys to nurturing our inner selves and fostering a deep connection with our own desires and aspirations.

Self-love requires perseverance, practice, and self-discovery. Let us approach this chapter with an open heart and allow ourselves to be completely embraced. By cultivating self-love, we establish the basis for a life replete with self-acceptance, happiness, and genuine fulfillment.

Together, let's embark on this transformative journey of self-love and unleash its immense power to shape our emotional well-being and create a life that truly reflects our true selves.

Prioritize Your Own Needs

It took me over 20 years to discover and practice self-love after growing up in an unhealthy environment. You might be wondering why it is so hard for so many individuals to simply love themselves. Psychologists might offer heaps of answers based on science and theory. However, after many conversations with friends and reflections on my own life, I have narrowed it down to two primary factors.

Human needs are ordered in tiers, often known as hierarchy, according to Maslow's Hierarchy of Needs (Maslow, 1943). The physiological demands are the most basic. In other words, people will prioritize survival basics such as food and shelter over higher-level needs. If someone feels unsafe and insecure for a variety of reasons, they are more inclined to secure themselves with more money or other types of security, such as working hard to secure one's job, saving money, and refusing to spend. Insecurity is a major impediment to self-love.

Another reason people struggle to love themselves is a lack of love as a child. If a child grows up in an unloving setting or with controlling parents, he or she will not learn unconditional love. In that way, this person's value system will convince her that she does not deserve self-love unless she has accomplished something. As a result, self-criticism and low self-esteem develop.

Self-reflection is an important step to evaluate whether you love yourself enough. Self-love is crucial to your wellness, including health, happiness and relationships. One will not be able to maintain healthy and long-lasting interpersonal relationships unless one loves and respects herself first. When one exercises self-love, she develops a strong sense of self-worth and self-compassion. Remember of not falling into the self-criticism spiral. Forgive yourself for not achieving a goal, give yourself enough sleep. Pamper yourself and grant yourself unconditional love.

Focus Internally not Externally!

My friend Martha is always unhappy. Her moods fluctuate, and she is constantly dissatisfied with the people around her. I am not a trained therapist; I can only talk to her as a friend, and her mood might weigh me down at times. Martha frequently complains that her partner is unconcerned about her sentiments and frequently forgets crucial dates. Martha is harsh on herself and frequently criticizing herself. She constantly compares herself to others and believes she is inferior. I'm sure you're starting to see the issue. There is no one else in the world who can always meet the expectations of others. If someone focuses on another person to provide her with pleasure and happiness, she will no doubt be disappointed. The main issue arises when someone doesn't love themselves and relies solely on seeking care and love from others. In this situation, there is a risk of draining the other person emotionally and depleting their own well-being in the process.

As a result, it is not uncommon to see that some people will live in a vicious cycle: meeting someone, falling in love, having some wonderful moments, then soon having quarrels and eventually breaking up. This type of person complains that they always meet the wrong person, have bad luck, etc. In fact, it is this self-defeating cycle that causes fate. If you find yourself continuously facing the same issue, it is time to sit back and reflect. There are many things in life that can be explained by one's own attitude. For example, when I was younger, I used to wonder why I always landed super-demanding jobs. Later, I get to learn that this is because I am a self-driven person, and it is in fact myself who is the root cause of overworking. I hope you will find this advice useful. Self-love is not the only answer to shaping your lifestyle, but it is a very important factor. You live a life you shape for yourself. If you want others to treat you a certain way, you need to treat yourself that way first. I am considering writing a book about self-love. This is too important, and I wish I could have learned about that earlier in my life.

Self-Care

What is the difference between self-love and self-care? How are these two concepts connected? Self-care is a manifestation of self-love.

As part of the research process of this book, I talked to some highly successful people, age between 60 – 90. They come from different backgrounds. Within this group, there is a mother of 7, also a highly successful businesswoman, a retired medical doctor, a music teacher who plays multiple instruments, and many more. I asked them, what is the number one advice you would give to a strong and independent woman who is living on her own in today's modern world? Interestingly, 9 times out of 10, the answer is "self-care".

People who are strong and independent, like most of us, share one common characteristic: self-reliance. We believe in our own capability, our resources, and our endurance in tackling various life challenges. We tend to put a lot on our own shoulders, and over time, it only takes one extra straw to kill the camel. The bare minimum is to eat well, give yourself enough sleep, and pamper yourself. Your body needs nutrients to function and enough rest to remain mentally robust. Your brain requires pleasure and happiness as incentives—chemically, that's called dopamine—to give the best of itself. Unless you have a clear mind, your energy level, your creativity, and your efficiency drop. Do not treat yourself like a robot. Pamper your own needs and practice self-care.

Contrarily, self-care is not equivalent to indulgence. It does not mean giving yourself whatever you want. Self-care involves discernment and judgment to evaluate what is right for yourself. You need to strike a balance between all your life choices. A general rule-of-thumb is that any behavior related to overdoing could be harmful. You are probably already thinking about overeating, shopaholics, workaholics, problem gaming, etc. But in fact, the list can be much broader. I once attended a training course about responsible gambling (don't worry for me; it is sponsored by the company I used to work for as part of the corporate social responsibility program). I discovered a set of screening questions that can be used to assess whether one has a tendency towards developing problem gambling behavior. Interestingly, I realized that some of these screening questions can be adapted and applied to other activities as well. By examining these questions, individuals can gain valuable insights into their own behaviors and tendencies in various areas of their lives. Below please find a list of self-screening questions. If you encounter issues with behaviors in life that you think you are overdoing and therefore self-harming, it is time to reflect and adjust.

1. Is the activity taking up a big chunk of your time and affecting your time to rest?
2. Does the activity affect your physical health or put strain on your health?
3. Is the activity affecting your relationships with family and people you love?
4. Is the activity affecting your finances so that you end up spending more than you have planned, or worse, more than you could afford?
5. Does your mind continue thinking about the activity, even during your full-time job or other activities?

6. Does the activity affect your quality at work or your concentration so that you cannot give the best of yourself?
7. Have you tried to exercise self-control, to regulate the behavior but failed before?
8. At least two of your close friends or family members have talked to you and reminded you that you may have issues that need to be fixed?

This is not a scientific examination, and there are no clear-cut scores with which you can self-diagnose problematic behavior. I suggest you ask yourself these questions as a self-reflection exercise to understand whether it is time to make adjustments to your behavior in order to exercise better self-care.

Childhood Experience

Most of us are aware that our early experiences might have long-term consequences for us. This is supported by schools of thought and empirical studies and is based on scientific research.

Childhood experiences are part of us, that impact who we are today. Apart from people who have come from abusive or severe circumstances that can create long-term trauma, most of us have had childhoods that are a mix of happiness and sadness, wonderful moments and bad times, things we love and things we loathe. We meet people we admire and respect, as well as people we hope we have never met. But aren't these the things that distinguish our lives? I'm sure you've heard of identical twins that live totally different lifestyles. Look it up, and you'll discover a lot of amazing examples of how, despite genetic and upbringing conditions, a person's attitude toward life influences what their adult life becomes.

Although it is well known that childhood experiences have a significant impact on a person throughout their life, it is important to realize that childhood only makes up a small portion of who we are. The way we live our lives is heavily influenced by our attitude toward them. Make no excuses; the past can serve as a useful guide. But we create our own narrative. For instance, a child of a problem drinker may tell himself that because he carries the addiction genes, becoming an alcoholic will be easy for him. However, another man may have claimed that having grown up with an alcoholic father has made him vow never to touch a drop of alcohol because he has witnessed the terrible effects it can have on a person's life and family. I'm trying to say that before the age of 18, we can blame our parents, family, upbringing, and fate. But as adults, we must navigate our own paths and refrain from preaching self-defeating doctrine to ourselves. Thinking that our intelligence, capability, and talents are innate is self-limiting. We must adopt a growth mindset and understand that we are in control of our destiny. Do not use our youth as a justification. Learn from the past and let the pleasant memories nourish our noble and contented spirits. On the other hand, let the painful memories act as our guardian angels, protecting us from harm with an immune system.

I recently met a young man who is deeply discontented with his own background. He gives me the impression that he is insecure. Throughout the brief conversation, he expresses his opinion of himself as being stupid and unattractive. He has few friends because he looks down on himself and avoids interacting with others. His cousin, a close friend of mine, told me that this young man frequently changes jobs. He avoids forming relationships with others because he believes that he is not likeable.

I do not know much about this guy's past, and I know I must not judge. Certainly, this young man's childhood experiences must have contributed to his behavior. Perhaps he experienced rejection or betrayal from those he trusted, leading him to avoid forming close bonds with others. However, it's important not to let past experiences limit our potential for growth and connection. I encouraged him to seek therapy or counseling, as I believe that could help him work through any unresolved issues and develop healthier patterns of relating to others. Ultimately, we all have the power to choose whether we allow our past experiences to define us or whether we use them as opportunities for growth and transformation. Don't let our childhood experiences limit us. As mentioned above, I believe people could conveniently put the blame on our parents, our family and our surroundings before the age of 18, but as we become adults, it is our responsibility to "make our own living and live our own lives". Stop blaming your parents.

Build Positive Self Image

Self-image refers to the way we mentally and emotionally perceive ourselves. It includes how we perceive our inner characteristics, capacities, and worth as well as how we perceive our appearances. Self-image is more than our self-projection of physical appearance. It also includes our beliefs, values, strengths, limitations, and feelings of identity, etc. Our experiences, society standards, cultural expectations, and individual judgments all have an impact on how we perceive ourselves.

Due to its direct relationship to our sense of self-worth and self-assurance, developing a positive self-image is very important. Having a positive self-image is the key to living a resilient and fulfilling life because it allows one to acknowledge and appreciate one's accomplishments and strengths, as well as accept one's flaws, and treat oneself with respect.

I must admit that I'm not a self-image engineering guru. I don't have a tried-and-true method to help you develop and improve yourself. But one thing I am certain of is that we must intentionally work to change our perspectives, attitudes, and behaviors such that they reflect the ideal version of ourselves.

How we perceive ourselves determines how others perceive us. If you believe you are unattractive and ungainly, you will demonstrate little confidence, causing others to lose faith in you. Let me share with you Sarah's story.

Sarah is a young woman who has always had trouble with how she sees herself. She thought she wasn't pretty or smart, so she didn't have much confidence in herself or what she could do. Sarah used to question what she was worth and was afraid to share her thoughts, fearing how others would judge her.

Because Sarah had a bad opinion of herself, she often held back in social settings. She spoke quietly because she was afraid her comments would be rejected. She avoided roles and opportunities that required her to be assertive. She kept thinking that she wasn't good enough.

A common friend introduced Sarah to me. I encouraged Sarah to share with me one thing that she is proud of. Sarah showed me some of her paintings, and I was thrilled by her talents. With Sarah's consent, I shared her drawings on social media. I received a lot of positive comments, saying how amazing Sarah's artworks were. Gradually, Sarah started to recognize her unique qualities.

As Sarah's view of herself changed, so did her confidence and the way she talked to other people. She started speaking up, telling people what she thought, and taking part in talks. People started to notice her real enthusiasm and honesty, which led to more opportunities, connections, and exposure.

Sarah's story showed us how important it is to have a good

picture of oneself. Projecting a positive self-image can be life changing. This is because our interpretation of ourselves affects how we connect with other people. Self-love is important and it can change a lot of things in life.

Self-Improvement

We all want to be the best version of ourselves, which entails ongoing learning and progress. Self-awareness is the first step toward self-improvement. So, the first question is, "Where do we start?" Remember that you don't want to set unrealistic expectations, or you'll be under constant stress. You must be aware of your own talents and flaws. You must be able to establish your values in life in order to identify areas for improvement that brings you real satisfaction.

Goal setting is another critical component. We must chart a course for our self-improvement journey. We must be able to quantify achievement and define what good looks like. It assists us in determining our goals and developing a strategy for success. But don't set an unattainable or overly broad goal for yourself. Any goal unachievable is not realistic. Pursuing an unattainable goal will result in frustration and exhaustion. Set both short-term and long-term goals for yourself and be sure to break them down into actionable steps. We must appreciate ourselves and celebrate tiny victories and accomplishments along the way in order to stay motivated.

Lifelong learning is crucial for personal progress, whether you are a young adult just starting out on your own or an experienced and autonomous individual. Adopting a growth attitude and putting forth effort to find opportunities for learning and self-education can be beneficial. Reading books, attending workshops or seminars, taking online courses, or engaging in meaningful interactions with people are all examples of this.

Lifelong learning is a journey. Persistence is required, and you will not see immediate results. We must form good habits. We must view self-improvement as an investment in which time, effort, and even money must be invested. The only distinction is that self-improvement is most likely the only guaranteed return on investment in our lives. Aside from studying, it is critical to develop other positive habits such as regular exercise, healthy nutrition, meditation or mindfulness techniques, journaling, and gratitude. All of these add up and will have a significant impact on our lives over time.

Self-improvement is more than just winning and achieving goals. Life is full of ups and downs, and self-improvement includes the ability to embrace failure, or, in other words, to create resilience. Accepting failure entails viewing setbacks as a learning opportunity. We must cultivate the mindset of viewing failure as a steppingstone to achievement. Remember that every setback you overcome brings you one step closer to success. In the face of hardship, building resilience allows us to adopt a growth mentality.

Remember that our lives are filled with surprises. There are both wonderful and bad things, happy and sad occasions. It is critical to surround yourself with positive people. This is critical for our personal development. Surround yourself with positive, like-minded people who can boost and motivate you. The more life experience you get, the more you will understand the value of mentorship. Being able to seek advice from individuals who have attained what we desire is a huge help, especially when we are in trouble.

Empower Yourself

You have the power to shape your own destiny and accomplish great things!

The foundation of empowerment is believing in yourself, which starts with acknowledging your self-worth and potential. I want to avoid cliché here, which I somewhat distaste. Like many of us, I have a collection of books on self-esteem and self-empowerment that I use as a cure for insomnia. They're not very helpful in making me a better person, but they sure do make great pillows!

So, let's change the angle by thinking about what "empower"

means to you. To me, it is to embrace the unique qualities that make us who we are and trust in our ability to navigate life's challenges and pursue our dreams. We all know that things will not change unless we do something. But we are humans, and human brains are wired to avoid danger. It is normal for us to feel hesitant about taking action when we are unsure about the outcome or when we have doubts about our own abilities. Our mind will give us a hazardous signal and stop us from making risky moves. You will feel "unsafe" moving forward, and it is absolutely normal. You are not a coward, but it is just your self-protection mechanism kicking in.

So how can we empower ourselves? My suggestion is to take calculated risks, then push forward so as to seek personal breakthroughs. It is not easy, of course. That "comfort zone" is being called a zone that is "comfortable", because leaving this zone makes us uncomfortable. Empowering ourselves means we need to step onto a horizon where we will feel uncomfortable, uncertain, and somewhat insecure.

The good news is that as you read this book, you will gain a cognitive understanding of how hesitancy and delay can be explained. You will comprehend why self-empowerment is counterintuitive in some manner. With this information, you are better equipped to achieve success. You will progressively cultivate a mindset of self-empowerment and make better use of your unique qualities. The same logic applies to physical training. You might not initially appreciate it. You used to experience muscle aches and fatigue after exercise, but you persevered because you knew it was beneficial for your health. As you began to see positive results, you gradually began to enjoy exercise.

Remember, you are capable of achieving amazing things if you believe in yourself. It is time to change some old habits in case you are used to negative self-talk. Start positive inner dialogue in shaping our self-perception. By challenging negative self-talk and embracing positive affirmations, we can reshape our mindset and cultivate a more nurturing and empowering inner voice. Through self-empowerment exercises and transformative mindset shifts, we will unlock the power of self-love to overcome self-doubt and build unwavering confidence.

LIFE SKILLS FOR WOMEN LIVING ALONE

Pursue Your Dream

"I yearned to accomplish the things I truly desired, yet found myself trapped in a cycle of doing things I never wanted to do. The longing to break free and live life on my own terms burned within me."

Samantha told me that she was in a poor mood and that her thoughts were jumbled. She invited me to join her for a drink after work. While I was sipping my glass of Cabernet Sauvignon, she made the above statement. I knew it wasn't the perfect timing for a joke, but I truly wanted to compliment her poetic expression.

I believe you might have shared similar feelings as Samantha, even if the feelings are not as intense. It is normal to feel discouraged from time to time. I believe most of you are doing full-time jobs, busy day after day, playing multiple roles as a co-worker, a subordinate, and even a supervisor. We need to fulfill our job duties and interact and collaborate with people, whether they like us or not. We need our job to support our lives— to put food on the table, pay rent, or pay mortgages. We sometimes stick with jobs for which we no longer have passion.

My view is that it is ok to be unhappy, but don't let that feeling drag you down. Instead, use that as a reminder. It is our sense of discontent that reminds us of our passion. When was the last time you felt passionate? What do you really want in life? I want to tell you that, despite some very rare situations, your dream and reality aren't totally contradicting each other. I have a friend who started learning ballet when she was 30. She could still master a lot of difficult techniques. I didn't write my first book until 2022, 25 years after I dreamed of becoming a writer. Now, take out a notebook (yes, trust me, pen and paper, in handwriting) and write down something that you want to do but have not yet accomplished. Write down what you need to do in order to get there. For example, when I plan to become a writer, I need to come up with the topic, conduct research, plan the outline, and then start writing the first chapter. Work out a plan and take baby steps. You will reach your destination only if you start to move towards your goals. Life is too boring without a dream to pursue. Don't let your future self down. You are the one to create your own legend and write your chapters.

Stand Up and Get Going

In the face of life's darkest days, I used to tell myself that I didn't care. I'd tell myself I was above the hurts and disappointments of the past. But I knew in my heart that I was fooling myself. When I finally reached the point where I could recount my experiences as though they were someone else's, I knew I had made it through the tough times.

There will be happy times and sad times throughout this journey we call life. The uncertainty of life is what gives it value. A new day brings fresh chances, and our past, for better or worse, will always be with us. Although the past might teach us valuable lessons, it cannot be changed. Though we may have lost out on wonderful love or suffered tragedy, we are better for it.

There is always give and take in life. We wouldn't be who we are now if we hadn't faced adversity and learned from our mistakes in the past. Everyone, including those who may have been our foes in the past, deserves to be appreciated. We grow stronger in the face of hardship. The trick is to pick ourselves back up when we fall and keep going.

I now believe that the best retribution is to create an amazing life of one's own making. Living a life full of happiness, prosperity, and fulfillment is the best way to provide joy to those who love us and pain to our enemies. This is a conviction I take with me wherever I go. Today I am a contented, prosperous, and self-sufficient individual. To those who have loved and supported me, I am eternally grateful, and to those who have sought to diminish and harm me, I give a respectful nod of appreciation. I feel bad because they tried to pull me down, but all that did was make me stronger and more determined to succeed.

Someone I used to work with tragically lost her fiancé in an accident the day he proposed to her. Sabrina lost her loved one the day they got engaged. Several of us tried to console her and offered our condolences. I only have a vague recollection of the words I said to Sabrina, but I ran across her two months later. She surprised me by being much cheerier and acting like she was doing well in her recovery from her loss. Sabrina thanked me, saying my words were very helpful and meant a lot to her. I was surprised by the impact my comments had on her, so I asked what stood out to her the most. "You told me that no one can help me except myself, regardless of what anyone else says. It's time to stand up and get going. Time is a great healer," Sabrina responded. She stated that she has been allowing her wound to heal since that day.

Friend, it's time for you to get up and begin moving. Accept the opportunities and setbacks that life provides. Drop what isn't helping you now and put your energy towards making your future a happy and successful one. You have it in you to triumph over adversity and lead a life of remarkable significance. Now that you've begun your adventure, know that I will be here to support you at every turn.

Chapter Six (Day 6) Summary

Chapter Six delves into the importance of self-love and emotional well-being, highlighting the need for self-belief, self-confidence, and setting clear boundaries. It emphasizes the value of resilience, positive thinking, and pursuing passions as key elements of personal growth and empowerment. This chapter encourages readers to reflect on their self-image, let go of past limitations, and embrace a fulfilling life. As we move into Chapter Seven, we will explore the exhilarating journey of discovering new hobbies and passions, finding fulfillment in personal pursuits, and unleashing our creative potential. It's time to ignite our curiosity and embark on a path of self-discovery and exploration.

Chapter Seven

LIFE PURSUITS AND PURPOSES

"Don't be afraid to give up the good to go for the great."
John D. Rockefeller

Welcome to Chapter Seven, which marks the beginning of a magnificent journey of introspection and self-improvement. When we have the luxury of being alone, we can follow our curiosities and whims into undiscovered areas of our imagination, creativity and fulfillment. In this chapter, you'll find a wealth of information that will help you explore latent skills, find fresh interests, and rekindle dormant passions.

Get buckled in and ready to take off on an exciting journey of introspection and the discovery of hidden interests. Let's get in and let your own strengths and passions shine!

Understand Yourself

This is based on David K. William's research on self-reflection (William, 2017). I've found them to be helpful whenever I'm at a crossroads from which to choose. I believe these will be useful for you too. Before we decide our next pursuit, it is important to have a deep level of self-understanding.

I recommend combining journaling with this set of questions. This allows you to periodically review your previous responses.

Assess yourself on the 30 questions below to learn more about who you are.

1. What is the true essence of my being?
2. What aspects of the future concern me the most?
3. If today were my last day on Earth, would I choose to engage in my current activities?
4. What fears have a stronghold on me?
5. Am I clinging onto something that I need to release?
6. If not now, then when will I take action?

7. What holds the utmost significance in my life?
8. How am I actively nurturing the things that hold the greatest importance to me?
9. What value do I bring to the world?
10. Have I recently undertaken any memorable endeavors?
11. Have I brought a smile to someone's face today?
12. What have I abandoned pursuing?
13. When was the last time I stepped outside of my comfort zone?
14. If I could impart one piece of advice to a newborn, what wisdom would I share?
15. What small act of kindness shown to me will forever remain etched in my memory?
16. How shall I live my life, knowing that death is inevitable?
17. What aspects of myself do I need to change?
18. Is it more crucial to love or to be loved?
19. How many of my friends would I trust with my life?
20. Who has had the most profound impact on shaping my life?
21. Would I break the law to protect a loved one?

22. Would I resort to theft to feed a starving child?
23. What is my deepest desire in life?
24. What does life beckon me to fulfill?
25. Which is more daunting: experiencing failure or never attempting?
26. If I set out to fail but end up succeeding, what have I truly accomplished?
27. When my life comes to a close, what is the one thing I want people to remember about me?
28. Does the opinion of others genuinely hold significant weight in defining my self-worth?
29. To what extent have I steered the course of my own life?
30. When everything is said and done, will I have spoken more than I have acted?

Remember that there are no right or wrong answers. I've discovered that my responses are inconsistent, as my worldview continues to change as I progress through life. Some aspects are relatively stable; these are my fundamental principles, which leave little room for negotiation. However, our perceptions and emotions could change as we gained experience. Others refer to this as maturity, and I call it evolution. For these reasons, I maintain a journal in which I date my responses. Typically, I don't answer all 30 questions, but instead select the ones that are most pertinent to my current state of mind. You will be thrilled to revisit the past and read your previous responses. This facilitates a greater level of self-understanding.

Your Inside Voice

Now, once you have your introspection answers written down, it is time to meditate on them.

Make some space that you can unwind in and enjoy. For maximum effect, I recommend doing it before bed (not on an empty stomach or one that is too full). When I really need to relax, I'll light an aroma candle or diffuse a calming essence oil like lavender or frankincense (or your favorite scent).

Turn down the lights and close your eyes to think deeply about your answers, your passion, and your desire. Consider what it is that truly drives you. In what ways do you hope to be remembered? To what end do you hope to contribute to society? The fact that I started life with nothing and have amassed such a large fortune fascinates me. Maybe you're thinking, "No, Winnie. I do not possess a lot". But picture yourself inside a safe house with a sturdy ceiling. Consider the delicious dinner that you just ate. Imagine the lotion or cream you just put on your skin. Some of the world's less fortunate may only be able to dream of having such comforts.

As I type these words, winter has settled in. The wind was howling outside, so I switched on the heating. Now I am home, protected behind my keyboard and listening to soft music. Counting my many blessings and remembering my good fortune. There are things I need to do, or else I won't be giving my life's worth to this wonderful world. Where do you stand?

Let Go of Your Worry

I have known the words of John 14:27, "Let not your heart be troubled," since I was a little child. Sometimes the simplest answer to a burden is, "Take your mind off it". It is time to listen to your heart. Prioritizing one's own happiness and dreams is essential in the quest for a life that matters. In the following sessions, we'll delve into a wide variety of activities that have the potential to improve our well-being on many levels. Engaging in these pursuits allows us to explore our interests and find new methods of expressing ourselves.

It is important to keep in mind, as we set out on this adventure together, that doing what makes us happy and chasing our ambitions is not something we should feel guilty about. Only when we are happy and content, we could make positive impact to those around us. This is due to the fact that we cannot give what we don't have.

Exercise and Sports

Engaging in regular exercise and participating in sports not only benefit our physical health but also contribute significantly to our mental wellness. It is a holistic approach to well-being that encompasses both body and mind. For those who enjoy the great outdoors, exploring outdoor sports can be a wonderful way to stay active while immersing oneself in nature's beauty.

It is important to acknowledge that as we age, our bodies may require different forms of exercise that are gentler on the joints and muscles. Instead of high-impact activities like jogging or running, opting for a brisk walk can still provide excellent cardiovascular benefits without placing excessive strain on the body. Listening to our bodies and choosing exercises that suit our individual needs is key to maintaining a sustainable fitness routine.

For those who thrive on social interactions and prefer sports that involve partners or teams, organizing activities with friends can be a fantastic way to stay motivated and accountable. By sharing a common goal, we can encourage and remind each other to prioritize our fitness journey. On the other hand, some individuals may find solace and peace in sports that can be enjoyed alone. Whether it's a solitary bike ride, a calming swim, or a meditative yoga session, these activities can provide a sense of personal space and introspection.

While embracing solo adventures can be exhilarating, it is important to prioritize safety. If venturing out for a hike, especially in remote areas with limited phone signal, it is advisable to have a hiking buddy or inform someone about your plans and estimated return time. This precautionary measure ensures that in the event of any unforeseen circumstances, there is someone aware of your whereabouts and able to offer assistance if needed.

Incorporating exercise and sports into our lives is not only about physical fitness; it is also about fostering mental health and achieving a sense of equilibrium. Whether you prefer the camaraderie of team sports or the solitude of solo activities, let us embrace the joy of movement and find the immense health and happiness benefits it provides.

Picking Up a Hobby

Pursuing a healthy hobby is not only a great way to spend your time but also holds the potential for personal growth, fulfillment, and even unexpected opportunities. Let me share with you the story of my good friend, Christina, who exemplifies the transformative power of picking up a hobby.

Christina has always been a cat-lover, deeply passionate about the well-being of feline friends. Seeking to enhance her own cats' grooming experience, she decided to learn pet grooming. Starting with a simple intention to groom her own four cats, Christina joined a professional course to refine her skills. Little did she know that this hobby would open up a world of possibilities for her.

As Christina honed her grooming abilities, she began offering her services to local animal shelters for free. Her genuine dedication and talent did not go unnoticed. Her exceptional grooming skills quickly gained recognition, and soon she found herself in high demand. Encouraged by the positive response and her growing passion, Christina took a leap of faith and opened her own pet grooming shop.

With time, Christina's business flourished, and her hobby turned into a thriving career. The joy and fulfillment she experienced from following her passion were immeasurable. Eventually, Christina made the bold decision to leave her previous job and pursue pet grooming full-time. Today, she is living her dream, doing what she loves, and making a positive impact in the lives of pets and their owners.

Just like Christina, I also discovered the incredible rewards of pursuing a hobby. Writing became my creative outlet, and I found immense satisfaction in penning down my thoughts and stories. The process of seeing my name on a book cover and connecting with readers worldwide brought me a sense of accomplishment and purpose. By following my passion, I embarked on a journey that opened up new dimensions and opportunities I never could have imagined.

So, my dear friend, I encourage you to embrace a healthy hobby that truly ignites your passion. You never know where it might lead you. Allow yourself to explore, learn, and grow in the pursuit of your interests. Follow the path that brings you joy, and who knows, one day it may turn into a remarkable journey that positively impacts your life and the lives of others.

Hobby and Volunteerism

When it comes to hobbies, the possibilities are truly limitless. It's a wonderful world out there, filled with opportunities to explore new interests and discover hidden talents. Whether you have a penchant for pottery, a desire to pick up a paintbrush, a yearning to learn a musical instrument, or a passion for drama and theater, there's something for everyone. Engaging in these creative pursuits brings joy and fulfillment and, at the same time, allows for self-expression and personal growth.

Imagine molding clay on a potter's wheel and shaping it into beautiful and unique creations. Pottery is both a therapeutic and meditative practice. It is a true fulfillment to turn artistic vision into tangible objects. Or if you are fascinated by the vibrant world of colors and textures, then allow yourself to capture emotions and stories on canvas through painting.

If music stirs your soul, why not consider learning to play a musical instrument? There are many choices, from piano to the melodic strumming of a guitar or the rhythmic beats of drums. Music has a magical ability to transport us to another realm. Playing an instrument brings personal joy and can also be a way to connect with others. I learned piano at the age of 35. Nowadays, I serve my church and play the piano during the Sunday service.

While pursuing your hobbies brings personal fulfillment, it's also important to consider how you can give back to society. Volunteerism is a wonderful way to make a positive impact and contribute to causes that resonate with you. In the United States, there are numerous nonprofit organizations

(NGOs) and organizations dedicated to various beneficiary groups and causes. For example, organizations like Feeding America work towards alleviating hunger and food insecurity. The American Red Cross provides support during emergencies and disasters, and Big Brothers Big Sisters of America pairs adult mentors with children in need of guidance and support. Exploring volunteer opportunities allows you to make a meaningful difference in the lives of others. Remember my friend Christina? She is an active volunteer at animal shelters.

Keep in mind that there is no limit to the variety of activities out there to explore. Follow your interests, explore new fields, and think about how you might make a difference in the world. You will meet a lot of like-minded individuals, too. Make your interests something that brings you pleasure, helps you develop, and has a beneficial effect on the world.

Religion Related Volunteerism

While I recognize that not everyone might benefit from church service, I can say that my own experiences there have been extremely rewarding. There is a vast landscape of opportunities available. You may or may not know that one does not need to be a believer in order to join in the volunteer work of a religious group.

A friend of mine recently joined her local church to assist with their annual holiday program for kids between the ages of seven and fourteen. Another one of my good friends routinely assists members of a religious organization with visits to senior centers. As part of her service, Fiona makes small talk with those speaking her native language. Since Fiona is a hotel employee, she needs to be on shift duty. Once, I had lunch with Fiona, and she casually said that the night before, she had worked the overnight shift, but that after getting off work, she immediately engaged in a volunteer activity. I asked her how she could have done it because I couldn't believe it myself. She answered, "The satisfaction I get from being able to help and contribute is as rejuvenating as an eight-hour sleep." I will not in any way encourage you to behave in similar manner. My argument is, volunteering is a very powerful mean in construction of life purposes.

Life Pursuit

It is up to us to maximize the value of this one precious gift of life. It's vital to keep in mind that our time on Earth is limited as we move through the various acts of our life. There is no telling how many years we have left, but we can be sure that each one is important. There is a certain number of years that are truly our own, even if we are blessed with a lengthy life.

When we look at the big picture of our lives, we see that there are times when our options are restricted. Our path is shaped by the innocence of childhood, the weight of adulthood, and the difficulties of old age. When our vitality and potential are at their highest, in our middle years, we should pause for thought.

I, too, have traveled the road of work dedication, putting in long hours to try to please other people. As the years passed, I began to wonder, "What am I here for?" What mark will I make on history? It jolted me awake, and I knew then that I had a responsibility to myself to find my life's purpose in something that would outlast my mortal coil.

My dear readers, if you have made this far and still reading, I hope you will take the time to learn more about who you are. Stop worrying about the little things and start asking, "What do I really want?" How do I find happiness and contentment in life? Pay attention to your inner voice; it holds the key to your happiness.

Don't let life pass you by since you're too busy with routine and responsibilities. Make an effort to discover your interests, develop latent skills, and follow your aspirations. Do what your heart tells you to do, whether that's making art, starting a business, volunteering for a cause you care about, or simply spending time with the people you care about.

Keep in mind that there is more to life than just earning a living. Making an impact while living a fulfilled life is at the heart of this concept. As we end this book, let's open the next one with a fresh feeling of purpose and resolve. In the time we have, may we make choices that bring us joy and satisfaction.

In closing, I hope that you, my dear friends, would recognize the value of each day and strive to live a life that matters to you. Follow your heart, and may your life be filled with love, laughter, and the realization of your deepest aspirations. Now is your chance to make a difference and leave a legacy of hope and positivity in the world. Take advantage of the moment; it is yours to enjoy.

Conclusion

We have set out on a voyage of transformation throughout this book, delving into various aspects of development, self-knowledge, and agency. We investigated the basics of protection, understanding the significance of both material and psychological safety. We next moved on to the arena of interpersonal relationships, where we learned the value of cultivating close friendships and the potency of human connection. From there, we dove deeper into the concepts of self-love and self-care, discovering ways to put our own needs first and adopt an optimistic perspective on ourselves. We broadened our horizons by taking up new activities and finding the satisfaction that comes from pursuing our passions. Finally, as we wrap up our travels, it's important to consider how our experiences thus far have informed our view of what it means to live a meaningful life.

We have learned, among other things, that life is short and full of surprises. We should value the years we have been given and use them wisely because time is limited. The truth is that our time on Earth is limited, regardless of how long we live. Subtracting the years spent sleeping and resting from the years spent dying, we find that our time left for significant endeavors is limited. It's a depressing concept, and it should cause us to take stock of our lives and our hopes and dreams.

Many of us spend our days working to pay the bills, tending to our families, and generally keeping up appearances. Sometimes we fail to take a step back and ask, "What is my purpose in life?" because we are too focused on the details. It was a question that struck me to my core, and I hope it does the same for you. We have to face the fact that our time here on Earth will run out. When it's all over, what legacy will we leave behind? Have we led lives of meaning and significance? Have we lived our lives to the fullest, bringing our special talents to the world?

Let us not forget the value of following our intuition as we wrap up this process of self-discovery. Let us resolve to find our true interests and dreams, for they are the key to a life well lived. I want you, dear reader, to welcome the unknown and explore the domain of possibilities. Do what you're interested in, take risks, and listen to the still, small voice within that tells you your true purpose.

Each of us has our own special way of adding to the overall beauty of life's great tapestry. We must spin our web with intention, honesty, and affection. This book is meant to be a gentle reminder that your life is a blank canvas, just waiting to be filled with the colors of your imagination. Embrace the boundless possibilities that await you and know that you are building a life of meaning and fulfillment with each step you take.

As we come to the end of this part of our journey, I want to thank you, dear reader, for accompanying me on this path of introspection and development. I greatly value your time and interest in this discussion. I hope that the insights you'll find here will serve you well as you pursue happiness and meaning. Always keep in mind that you are the master of your own fate and can design a future that brings you happiness. Have faith in yourself, have faith in your path, and be open to the magic that happens when you tune in to your heart.

THANK YOU

Dear Reader,

I want to start by expressing my deepest appreciation for choosing my book as your companion in this journey. It warms my heart to know that you entrusted me with your time and allowed my words to resonate with you. I sincerely hope that this book has brought you joy and proven to be a valuable resource.

My intention in writing this book was to share my experiences, and to provide you with practical advice and encouragement. I genuinely hope that it has served its purpose and offered you solace and guidance.

Your support and feedback mean the world to me. As an independent author, I rely on readers like you to continue pursuing my passion and sharing my knowledge. If you could take a moment to share your thoughts on this book, whether through a review on Amazon or sending email to me directly, it would be an immense help. Your feedback helps me improve my writing and subsequently assists others in making informed decisions.

Rest assured that I will carefully read and consider every review and take your thoughts to heart. Your opinions, suggestions, and insights are incredibly valuable to me, as I strive to create meaningful books that resonate with my readers.

I also want to remind you to claim your bonus gift, which awaits you as a token of my gratitude. Please refer to the instructions on page 7 to access it.

Once again, thank you from the bottom of my heart for your support. I genuinely hope to connect with you soon and continue building a friendship through our shared love for books and the journey of living alone.

Warm regards,

Winnie Gold

    Leave a review on Amazon US
    Leave a review on Amazon UK

ABOUT THE AUTHOR

Winnie Gold is an independent person who finds solace and happiness in her own consciousness. As a dedicated introvert, she cherishes the serenity of her own company and revels in the joy of reading and writing. It is through these passions that she has discovered a profound connection to the world around her, transcending the need for spoken words or face-to-face interactions.

In her earlier years, Winnie embarked on a professional journey in the dynamic field of public relations within the hospitality industry. Surprisingly, for an introvert, she excelled in this realm of "professional extroversion." Through her work, she honed her communication skills and learned the art of connecting with people from all walks of life. This experience allowed her to understand the power of genuine human connection and the importance of empathetic storytelling.

Now, as an indie author, Winnie has found her true calling.

She embraces the written word as a means to bridge the gaps between individuals across the globe. Winnie's ability to share her experiences, wisdom, and knowledge brings her immense joy, and she hopes that her words will resonate deeply with those who read them.

Drawing from her background in public relations, Winnie skillfully crafts narratives that engage, enlighten, and empower her readers. With each word she writes, she aspires to offer solace, guidance, and a sense of belonging to those who may feel the weight of solitude. Her desire is to provide a literary haven where individuals can find inspiration, courage, and the tools to navigate the challenges of living alone.

Discover the world of Winnie Gold, where words become vessels for connection, understanding, and the timeless exploration of the human spirit.

References

Abazov, R. (2022, October 24). *5 ways to improve creative thinking.* https://www.topuniversities.com/blog/5-ways-improve-your-creative-thinking

Ackerman, C.E. (2017, December 18). *87 Self-reflection questions for introspection (+exercises).* Positive Psychology. https://positivepsychology.com/introspection-self-reflection/

Bates, S.M. (2012, November 11). *Check yo' self: an exercise in self-reflection.* Hello Giggles. https://hellogiggles.com/check-yo-self-an-exercise-in-self-reflection/

Baumeister, R.F., Tierney, J. (2011). *Willpower: rediscovering the greatest human strength.* Penguin Press

Bradshaw, F. (2021, July 7). *How to turn negative thoughts into positive actions.* Mind Tools. https://www.mindtools.com/blog/how-to-turn-negative-thoughts-into-positive-actions/

Carmbody J. Baer, R. (2008). Relationships between

mindfulness practice and levels of mindfulness, medical and psychological symptoms and well-being in a mindfulness-based stress reduction program. *Pubmed 31*, p. 22–33. https://www.researchgate.net/publication/5946075_Relationships_between_mindfulness_practice_and_levels_of_mindfulness_medical_and_psychological_symptoms_and_well-being_in_a_mindfulness-based_stress_reduction_program

Cherry, K. (2023, April 4). *Introspection and how it is used in psychology research*. Very Well. https://www.verywell.com/what-is-introspection-2795252

Corley, T. (2016). *Change your habits change your life*. North Loop Books.

Dahl, M. (2017, March 27). *Sometimes 'introspection' is you just making stuff up*. Science of Us. http://nymag.com/scienceofus/2017/03/sometimes-introspection-is-you-just-making-stuff-up.html

Dweck, C. (2006). *Mindset: the psychology of success*. Random House

Eurich, T. (2017, June 2). *The right way to be introspective (yes, there's a wrong way)*. TED. https://ideas.ted.com/the-right-way-to-be-introspective-yes-theres-a-wrong-way/

Hamre, E. (2020, February 10). *How learning new skills rewire your brain.* https://medium.com/skilluped/how-learning-new-skills-rewire-your-brain-af08f0aee43

Henderson, L. (2022, May 28). *3 Ways to change your mindset for success and happiness.* Fast Company. https://www.fastcompany.com/90755578/3-ways-to-change-your-mindset-for-success-and-happiness

Hogarty, S. (2022, August 23). *Growth mindset: definition, characteristics and examples. Are your abilities set in stone? Or can they be improved? Here is how a growth mindset can help.* We Work. https://www.wework.com/ideas/professional-development/business-solutions/growth-mindset-definition-characteristics-and-examples

Joseph, S. (2023, February 19). *The power of surrounding yourself with people who are doing better than you.* LinkedIn. https://www.linkedin.com/pulse/power-surrounding-yourself-people-who-doing-better-than-scott-joseph/?trk=pulse-article_more-articles_related-content-card

Maier, S. (2018). *100 Great mindset changing ideas*. Marshall Cavendish Business

Maslow, A.H. (1943). "A Theory of Human Motivation". In Psychological Review, 50 (4), 430-437.

McGonigal, K. Ph.D. (2012). *The willpower instinct: how self-control works, why it matters, and what you can do to get more of it*. Penguin Group

McLeod, S. (2023, February 15). *Wilhelm Wundt: Father of Psychology*. Simply Psychology. https://www.simplypsychology.org/wundt.html

Mosley, L. (2016. March 18). *The importance of understanding personality type in the workplace*. LinkedIn. https://www.linkedin.com/pulse/importance-understanding-personality-type-workplace-lauren-copeland/

Neuroplasticity. (2019, October 2). Psychology Today. https://www.psychologytoday.com/us/basics/neuroplasticity

Newman, K. (2016, November 9). *Five science-backed strategies to build resilience*. Greater Good Magazine. https://greatergood.berkeley.edu/article/item/

five_science_backed_strategies_to_build_resili
ence

A quote by Charles A. Jaffe. (n.d.). Goodreads. https://www.goodreads.com/quotes/258944-it-s-not-your-salary-that-makes-you-rich-it-s-your

A quote by John Locke. (n.d.) Brainyquote. https://www.brainyquote.com/quotes/john_locke_151482

A quote by Sir Brian Appleton. (n.d.). https://weeklysafety.com/safety-quotes/management-quote

A quote by Thomas Jefferson. (n.d.). Pinterest. https://www.pinterest.com/pin/638807528364493293/

A quote by Helen Keller. (n.d.). Brainyquote. https://www.brainyquote.com/quotes/helen_keller_384608

A quote by Jennifer Louden. (n.d.). Pinterest. https://www.pinterest.com/pin/245375879684597953/

A quote by John D. Rockefeller. (n.d.). Brainyquote. https://www.brainyquote.com/quotes/john_d_rockefeller_119902

Ravishankar, R.A, Alpaio, K. (2022, August 30). *5 ways to set more achievable goals*. Harvard Business Review. https://hbr.org/2022/08/5-ways-to-set-more-achievable-goals

Sabarich, C. (2023, March 9). *10 positive affirmations for success that will change your life.* Life Hack. https://www.lifehack.org/489003/10-positive-affirmations-for-success-that-will-change-your-life

Scott, S. (2022, November 4). *107 Positive affirmations for success in life.* Happier Human. https://www.happierhuman.com/affirmations-success/

Symth, B. (2020, January 6). *How to positively receive negative feedback.* Skill Path. https://skillpath.com/blog/how-to-positively-receive-negative-feedback#:~:text=Be%20quiet%20and%20listen%20to,feedback%20in%20a%20positive%20light

William, D.K. (2017, November 14). *30 Thought-provoking questions you should ask yourself every day.* Life Hack. https://www.lifehack.org/articles/communication/30-thought-provoking-questions-you-should-ask-yourself-every-day.html

Wood, D. (2013, September 29). *The lost art of introspection: Why you must master yourself.* Expert Enough. http://expertenough.com/2990/the-lost-art-of-introspection-why-you-must-master-yourself

Woronock, M. (2019, June 19). *The power of self-reflection: 10 questions you should ask yourself.* Life Hack. https://www.lifehack.org/articles/communication/the-power-self-reflection-ten-questions-you-should-ask-yourself.html

www.ingramcontent.com/pod-product-compliance
Lightning Source LLC
Chambersburg PA
CBHW031106080526
44587CB00011B/850